H✿ME
made simple®

H❀ME
made simple®

fresh ideas
to make your own™

the experts at home made simple

st. martin's griffin ⚏ new york

www.stmartins.com

Design by Ralph Fowler / rlfdesign

Interior and cover custom photographs by OMS Photography

Credits for material used in this book:

Procter & Gamble
   Juan Fernando Posada; Scott Lazarczyk; Diane Hensley, Scott Mautz, Melanie Allen, Jennifer Trump

Discovery Communications
   Eileen O'Neill; JP Stoops; Grant McAllister

Barefoot Proximity
   Amanda Brown; Jodi Greene; Leslie Kiefaber; Meg Pautke; Susan Davidson

Barefoot Proximity Editorial Contributors
   Rachel Kirkwood; Jacob Perry; Amanda Stout; Claire Keys

Barefoot Proximity Design Contributors
   Beth Lintz; Tom Bolton; Kat Jenkinson; Meggie Schroth

ISBN 978-0-312-64147-4

contents

welcome

For years Home Made Simple has helped make your home a place you love to live in. We've reveled in bringing you ideas and products that simplify, beautify, and inspire the moments you create there. That's why we're so happy to introduce a collection of those ideas that we've gathered just for you.

Home Made Simple is a home-reference guide heaped with fresh inspirations, simple how-tos, and ways to infuse these with your personal touch. In these pages you'll find tips, projects, and recipes that will help you create a home that is truly your own. We even encourage you to personalize this book by jotting down your thoughts in the work spaces throughout!

Thank you for inviting us into your life. We hope this collection serves you well as an everyday reminder to be inspired, live simply, and love each moment at home.

Enjoy,
The Experts at
Home Made Simple

organized life

store. streamline. *harmonize.*

Creating order out of the clutter and chaos of daily life is truly a rare gift. For the lucky few who have a natural knack for organizing, everything has its place (and everything is labeled, coordinated, and uncluttered). But for most of us it's the little victories that really count and make our lives easier.

We know how important it is to have a comfortable, organized home without spending every moment making it that way. That's why the pages in this chapter are brimming with fresh and easy ideas that fit into your home in ways that are manageable, empowering, and true to life.

Our lives and homes are filled with little challenges and puzzles that need to be solved. Hopefully, some of the organizing solutions we've discovered along the way will help inspire you to streamline your home and create harmony and happiness that is all your own.

clean and clear routines

Everyone knows the basics, but sometimes it is hard to tell (or remember) how often items in the home need to be cleaned. For your most-often-overlooked and baffling cleaning projects, here are step-by-step instructions on what to do and how.

cleaning routine guide

Have you ever wondered when was the last time a certain item in your home was cleaned? Or even how often something needs a good scrubbing? Use the guide on pages 4–5 to keep track of all the whens and wheres of your cleaning routine. You can even fill in your own time reminders so you don't forget when a certain cleaning is due.

how-to: **blinds**

The best way to keep your blinds clean is to dust them about every month. Something so small can make a big difference over time. The less dust and dirt you let build up, the less often you'll have to give them a deep clean. If you dust them regularly, you'll need to wash your blinds only every two to four years. When it gets to be that time, follow these simple steps to get them squeaky clean again. All you need is an all-purpose cleaner, a bucket of warm water, a sponge, and a large bath towel.

- Close and remove your blinds. To remove, simply pull up the tabs on each end and slide the blinds out. Lay them out in a flat, open area, such as your driveway, yard, or kitchen floor.

- Lay the bath towel under your first set of blinds. Spray generously with the cleaner and let sit for several minutes.

- With a damp sponge, wipe the slats in a horizontal motion until all the dust and dirt buildup is wiped clean. For heavier dirt, scrub the blinds gently with a soft-bristled brush, also in a motion parallel to the slats. Wipe with plain water. If you are cleaning your blinds out-

your cleaning routine

	Every Day	Weekly	Monthly	Seasonally	Yearly

Kitchen	Do dishes
	Wipe counter-
	  tops and table
	_____
	_____
	_____
	_____
	_____
	_____
		Organize fridge
		  and check for
		  old food
		flush garbage
		  disposal
		Wipe appliances
		Clean out
		  microwave
		Mop floors
		_____
		_____
			Change baking
			  soda in fridge
			_____
			_____
			_____
			_____
			_____
			_____
				Organize freezer
				  and check for
				  old food
				Clean oven
				Organize pantry
				  and check for
				  old food
				Wipe out fridge
				Wipe backsplash
				Wipe walls
					Wash ventilation
					  hood filters
					Wipe out
					  cabinets
					_____
					_____
					_____
					_____

Living Room	_____
	_____
	_____
	_____
	_____
	_____
	_____
	_____
		Organize books
		  and magazines
		Organize toys
		Fluff and flip
		  cushions
		Launder throw
		  blankets
		_____
		_____
		_____
			_____
			_____
			_____
			_____
			_____
			_____
			_____
				Wipe walls
				Clean fireplace
				  screen
				_____
				_____
				_____
				_____
				_____
					_____
					_____
					_____
					_____
					_____
					_____
					_____

Bathroom	_____
	_____
	_____
	_____
	_____
	_____
	_____
	_____
		Clean sinks
		Wipe mirrors
		Clean showers
		  and tubs
		Clean toilets
		Mop floors
		Launder linens
		_____
		_____
			Scrub or bleach
			  grout
			_____
			_____
			_____
			_____
			_____
				Wipe walls
				Organize
				  cabinets
				_____
				_____
				_____
				_____
					_____
					_____
					_____
					_____
					_____
					_____

	Every Day	Weekly	Monthly	Seasonally	Yearly
Bedrooms	Make beds	Change sheets Fluff pillows and comforters Wipe mirrors		Dry clean duvets and mattress pads Flip mattresses	
All Around	Pick up	Vacuum floors and steps Dust or vacuum furniture Dust and wipe electronics Empty trash Wipe smudges off glass surfaces	Launder rugs Clean radiators or vent covers Vacuum baseboards Dust window sills	Wipe photo and art frames Wash out trash cans Clean switches and outlets Dust ceiling fans Wipe front door Sweep out fireplace	Wipe trim Flush drains with vinegar Put away old magazines Clean leather furniture

side, you can rinse the cleaner away with hose water and then shake excess water from the blinds. If you are inside, use a sponge and bucket of water. Note: For wooden blinds and fabric shades, do not use water or cleaner because dampness can warp the wood slats and stain the fabric material. Instead, wipe with a soft dust cloth or sweep with a vacuum cleaner brush attachment.

- Reverse the slats and repeat.

- Allow the blinds to dry for several hours before rehanging.

how-to: **fireplace**

A warm, welcoming fire will make any room cozy. Unfortunately, fireplaces are messy to work with because they're hard to keep ash- and soot-free. To clean your fireplace, gather these supplies: a drop cloth, a newspaper, a wire brush, a fireplace shovel, a fireplace broom, a large lined trash can, a scrub brush, a bucket, glass cleaner, rubber gloves, and paper towels.

- Consider wearing old clothing that you don't mind ruining—just in case the soot stains them.

- Use a wire brush to remove excess soot from the andirons and grate. Set them aside out of the way, where you can clean them later, outside.

- Now focus on the fireplace. Put down a drop cloth where you can kneel. Place your trash can within arm's reach. Lay a drop cloth on any flooring that is near the fireplace. Spread newspaper on top of the drop cloth at the hearth and inside the fireplace area.

- Scoop up the ashes with a fireplace shovel and move them into the trash can. Be careful not to stir the ashes; they can spread through the air and stain nearby carpeting and upholstery. Sweep up the loose dust.

- Use a wire brush to loosen soot from the walls of the fireplace, starting at the top. Lift the newspaper and fold up the soot inside it. Place it carefully into the trash can.

- In a bucket, mix one gallon of warm water with one cup of bleach. Wearing rubber gloves, use a scrub brush and the water to scrub soot and creosote off the walls and floor of the fireplace. (Some

> Depending on how often you use your fireplace, you should have it inspected and swept by a professional chimney sweep company every one to three years.

areas in older fireplaces may be stained black from years of heat exposure.) Then gather the wet newspapers and use them to soak up extra liquid. Discard these newspapers.

- Clean the fireplace grates with the same mixture and scrub brush.

- Finish off the freshly cleaned fireplace interior with a clean exterior. Use glass cleaner and newspapers to clean glass doors.

how-to: **drip coffeemaker**

Cleaning your coffeemaker is not hard to do, but it can be hard to remember to clean! Once you do, you'll notice how much fresher your coffee tastes. All you need is white vinegar and water.

- Fill the pot with one part white vinegar to two parts water or half vinegar and half water, depending on the amount of buildup in your particular machine. Do not use baking soda because it will clog and ruin the appliance.

- Place a filter in the filter cup, pour the solution where you usually put water, and let the liquid run through the machine.

- Discard the filter and mixture.

- Run plain water through the coffeemaker twice to rinse away any remaining vinegar.

- Run your filter cup and pot through the dishwasher.

> **Here's a great natural way to clean and refresh your coffeemaker. Fill it one-third of the way with ice. Then add 2 tablespoons of table salt and a lemon wedge. Stir and watch as the stains disappear. Rinse with water, and you'll have a clean, great-smelling coffeemaker.**

scrumptious spice storage

Spices make your favorite dishes irresistible. That is why it is so important to keep them fresh and organized. Find out if your spices are as flavorful as they could be and how to make your collection more delicious tasting—and looking—than ever before.

spice freshness 101

Understanding how spices work is the first step toward successful spice storage. Here are a few facts:

- Let's start with what gives spices their flavor. Inside are oils that, when heated, flavor the food you cook them with.

- Spices lose their flavor over time as the oils evaporate. Sunlight and heat speed up this process, drying out the spices and causing them to lose their flavor more quickly.

- Overall, spices last longest in cool, dry spots.

- Some professionals say that even in the best conditions, most spices last only a few months.

> **Try a micro-zester to grind whole spices as you need them. This helps your spices taste bolder and last longer, too.**

how-to: **buy and store**

Professionals recommend that you buy fresh, whole spices when possible. Like coffee beans, they keep their flavor longer when stored whole. Many markets have spice stations where you can measure out the amount you need. Then you can take your spices home and put them in a container of your choice. This approach to spice stocking is often less expensive since you don't have to buy more than you can use before they go stale. Plus, you save on paying for a new container each time!

If you do buy your spices preground and prepackaged, try to find those packed in metal tins or tinted glass rather than clear jars, which let in harmful light.

are yours safe?

Are you storing your spices where sunlight or heat can get to them? If so, don't feel bad—you're not alone! Many people keep their spices in glass containers out on their counter by the stove. Unfortunately, this is where they're exposed to the most sunlight from windows and lots of heat from the stovetop. Fortunately, smarter spice storage is only a few steps away.

convert your rack

If you have a spice rack that sits on the counter, there's no need to throw it away! Simply paint the glass jars with chalkboard paint. This way, harmful light is blocked, and you have a new way to mark which spice is in which jar. Don't forget to write the date on a jar you've filled with fresh spices, too, so you know when it gets old. Simply move the rack as far away from heat sources as possible.

create a jar collection

If you'd prefer to keep your spices tucked in a cabinet, clear glass will work just fine. Create an eclectic collection of glass jars. Start by keeping old spice jars instead of pitching them with the old contents. Simply soak off the label and then fill the jar with loose spices as you buy them. You can use other kinds of glass containers, too, such as pimiento, olive, and small jelly jars. The wider mouths are often easier to dip into with your measuring spoon anyway.

To help you see all your spice options at once, consider investing in a tiered spice shelf to place in your cabinet. They're inexpensive, widely available, and help you avoid having to dig to the back of the cupboard.

make a magnetic spice board

If you don't have a spice rack, here's an organizational system you may like to do yourself (DIY). In a few steps you can create an easily accessible magnetic spice board. For this project you can repurpose your own spice tins and look for more at thrift stores and antique shops to add to your collection.

Materials

Particle board	Permanent markers
Magnetic paint	Round magnets
Paintbrushes	Super glue
Acrylic paint in assorted colors to complement your kitchen	Power drill
Square spice tins	Screws

Instructions

1. Paint your particle board with the magnetic paint. A couple of coats will increase the board's magnetic strength.
2. With your acrylic paint, cover the tins in colors that complement your kitchen.
3. Using your markers, write the names of the different spices on each tin.
4. On the back of each tin, affix a magnet with glue.
5. Drill screw holes into your board and place the screws on the wall of your choice.
6. Hang the board on the wall.
7. Fill your tins with spices and place them on the board.

enjoy cooking in an efficient kitchen

Whether you are cooking a big family feast for dozens or a simple every-day dinner, creating a clean and organized kitchen space can make all the difference. A well-laid-out kitchen makes time spent cooking a more efficient and enjoyable experience for you.

start with the fridge

Before you do anything else, clean out and organize your refrigerator so you have plenty of room for all your meal ingredients. Start by grouping together the ingredients that you'll be using, but be sure to leave plenty of room for the items that you'll be buying for your meal as well as any dishes or drinks your guests may bring. Don't forget to anticipate left-overs, too.

organize your tools and spaces

Look at your work spaces and the organization of your kitchen items. Are there appliances crowding your countertops? Do you have to dig through a disorganized drawer to find utensils? It may be a good time to sort your cooking tools.

- **Start with a clean and organized work space.** Be sure all your kitchen surfaces are wiped down and clutter-free. Whether you have a large countertop to work on or very limited space, designate at least one area to keep clear for food preparation at all times.

- **Create a kitchen work triangle.** For an efficient kitchen, set up three main work spaces:

  1. Preparation area

  2. Cook and serve area

  3. Clean-up area

work space

Create a quick sketch of your kitchen work triangle, including your preparation, cook-and-serve, and clean-up areas. What appliances, utensils, and ingredients go in each?

The kitchen triangle is a system that connects your refrigerator, sink, and stove to create a sense of fluidity as you move about the kitchen. Organizing your most important tools and ingredients around these key kitchen zones will help you take fewer steps to get to the items you need for preparation and cooking. Try keeping useful items in each zone; for example, storing your dishes and silverware between your cook-and-serve and clean-up areas will help you get dinner to the table faster and the dishes can be put away after washing more efficiently.

getting ready to cook

Before a special holiday meal or even when planning your weekly dinners, take some time to organize your recipes, cook times, ingredients, and tools. These tips will help get you started on a path to efficient cooking in your kitchen:

- **Give a quick kitchen tour.** Having helping hands in the kitchen can be wonderful, but those who are new to your kitchen or organization style may have a few questions. Giving your guests a quick kitchen tour or setting out cooking tools and ingredients before cooking starts will help everyone cook smoothly together.

- **Sharpen your knives.** Keeping your knives sharp is safer and will cut your preparation time in half. When a knife is sharp, it requires less force to make cuts and is much easier to control. As always, store sharp knives separately from other utensils in a knife block or rack, to prevent cutting yourself or nicking other silverware.

- **Don't crowd the oven.** If you need to cook several side dishes at once, choose casseroles that fit into your oven with spaces in between and stagger pans on upper and lower racks. Good airflow in the oven allows food to cook much faster and more evenly, so avoid covering racks with foil or trying to cook too many dishes at once.

create a welcoming work space

Your desk, your home office, your work space—whatever you call it and wherever it is, this is the area that helps you keep your life organized or inspires you to be creative. But the household command center doesn't have to be all business. A comfortable work area is more calming and efficient. Use these helpful ideas for creating a welcoming and organized work space in your home.

setting up a comfortable office

- **Choose your space.** Whether you have a whole room or just a corner in the kitchen for your office, try to organize your desk and chair for optimal comfort. If you're able to face a window or a door, you won't feel as confined in your work area, and you'll have more natural light and space. Be sure you set up your desk and wall organization, such as calendars and shelving, so you can easily reach the items you need.

- **Find the right chair.** Your office chair is definitely an item that should favor function over style. If you don't have a comfortable chair with good support and movement, you won't be able to work efficiently or sit for extended periods if you need to.

- **Illuminate your area.** Lighting is another important part of your work environment. Overhead lights can be harsh or create a glare. A small lamp adds warmth while illuminating your desk with inviting light. Good lighting also prevents eyestrain, which will tire you out faster.

- **Have enough storage.** Consider how you'll use your work space and be sure to have enough storage to suit your needs. If you like to read, line a wall with bookshelves. If you have a lot of paperwork to store, invest in a large filing cabinet or a series of matching file boxes.

inviting ways to organize

Even if you already have an organization system for your desk, there are ways to make it more welcoming.

- Try to keep a section of the main desk surface free and open at all times. That way, even if you have files or shelves on your desk, you'll always have a clean, uncluttered spot to sit down and get to work.

- Practice cord management. Tack unsightly cords up under the desk or hide them under a small rug to prevent tripping or getting your chair caught. If you have a file system or mailboxes on your desk, you can hide cords under or behind these items as well.

- Add some personalization to your organization tools. Use memorable photos of your family members to decorate mailboxes and use folders, shelves, and containers in colors that will energize and inspire you instead of the usual blacks, browns, and manilas.

adding special touches

Having items around your desk that make you feel happy, encouraged, and motivated will make your tasks more manageable and keep you moving forward toward your goals.

- Evaluate the artwork in your home office or work area. If you don't feel it's inspiring you, remove it and replace it with artwork or images that make you feel energized and happy.

- Place a small leafy green plant on your desk and keep it well maintained and healthy. This brings natural beauty and life into your work space. To get tips for choosing a pretty plant that also helps keep the air in your area clean and fresh, see Breathe Easy at Home on page 210.

- Don't add more clutter to your desk, but a few fun knickknacks, such as a framed postcard or an award certificate, will remind you of a memorable vacation or a special achievement and put a smile on your face.

> Paint an accent area in your work space. Use chalkboard or magnetic paint to create a fun surface for writing, drawing, or tacking up ideas and inspiration.

- Include calming elements like a scented candle, stress ball, or fresh flowers that can help ease mental strain.

- Try to make your organization materials decorative, too, if you use your office or work space for crafts or scrapbooking. Use containers, bins, and holders that allow you to see what's inside so you can easily access what you need. You can also decorate your boxes and bins with items you use for your hobby. Seeing your colorful ribbons and pretty accents all organized and ready to use will help inspire you to be creative.

check out a personalized library

Your assortment of reading material is a reflection of your personal interests, aspirations, and worldviews. Showcase it as thoughtfully as you would any other collection. Try these ideas for organizing your personal library in ways as unique as your book collection itself.

stylish stacking

Brainstorm creative ways to organize your library. Here are a few ideas to get you started:

- **Reading Rainbow:** One creative and colorful idea for personalizing your library is to sort it by the color of the book spines. Forget the Dewey decimal system; start with the purples and work your way to purplish blues, then blues, and so on through the color spectrum. From afar you'll have a rainbow of books that bring cheer to your shelf.

- **Distinctive Sorting:** Divide your reading material by interest or topic and create purposeful piles of books and magazines in nooks throughout your home. Arrange each stack artistically, with larger books at the base and smaller ones on the top. Place your favorite knickknack on top.

  For example, if you are a nature lover, you may want to group your bird books or collection of campfire stories by a window seat overlooking your backyard. Finish the stack with an animal figurine or geode rock that symbolizes the nature books beneath it. You can also keep a pair of binoculars there, too, for easy nature observation between reads.

  If you love fiction, consider filling a basket with your favorite novels and placing it beside your coziest reading chair. It is a great place to keep your library books together, and you can even use the basket to tote them back and forth.

- **Colorful Cookbooks:** Instead of tucking them away, keep your cookbooks out where they can be celebrated. Since cookbooks often come in a particularly bright array of colors, they may add a new vibrancy to your kitchen. They are also a great way to show off your tastes. Try them in an open bookcase or a floating shelf near your most used counter. Not only will your recipes be easier to reach, but your collection will serve as an everyday reminder to break out of your routine and try different dishes.

easy id labels on books

Labels are another personal touch that help keep your library organized. They remind borrowers where to return the item, too.

You can create your own label design or use our designer template. Simply make color copies, cut them out, and affix one to the inside front

FROM THE
LIBRARY OF

homemadesimple.com

cover of each book. To make sure that your labels will last for years, use acid-free archival glue for securing them to your book covers. It is available in the scrapbook supply aisle of your local craft store. Because it will never yellow or disintegrate the label, you'll be able to pass your favorite stories on for generations to come, complete with the history behind them.

tips for tracking

If you and your friends swap books frequently, make it easier to remember where borrowed books went by creating a journal to catalog "checkouts." You can also use this journal to make notes about books you're borrowing from others so you don't forget which one goes back to where.

from the library of

homemadesimple.com

organized stationery solutions

Make staying connected with friends and family simple and organized. Keeping your collection of stationery streamlined is one of those small details that can make a big difference. Being prepared can also help you cut the expense of buying pricey cards and paper in a hurry. Learn to think ahead and create an organized stationery kit so that you're ready for last-minute birthday cards and quick thank-you notes at a moment's notice.

the write way

Even though there are many ways to communicate with friends and family these days, there are still occasions that call for the personal touch of a handwritten letter, note, or card. Plus, well-timed correspondence penned on unique paper expresses your thoughtfulness in a way that e-mail simply can't.

A stationery kit is a thoughtful gift idea for anyone who loves collecting stationery and writing personal letters—or if you just want to encourage someone special to write more!

create your kit

Organizing your stationery not only makes it easier to find what you need instead of searching for an envelope, postage stamp, or the perfect card, but it also makes staying in touch a fun and effortless experience.

storage solutions

- **Portable:** Repurpose an accordion file organizer as a simple portable solution that will fit easily on a shelf or a desk or in a drawer. Keep all your stationery essentials in each of the pockets, and if you have tabs, label them so you can quickly find what you need. If you're repurposing the folder and the tabs already have writing on them, cover them with sticker tabs or cut and glue colorful pieces

of construction paper onto the existing tabs. Use different colors to create a code for your pockets.

- **Desktop:** For an easy access desk, table, or countertop solution, repurpose a dish rack to separate your stationery materials into sections. You can also store pens, pencils, stamps, and other accessories in the utensil holders. If you have a favorite collection of stationery, this is a fun way to show it off—plus, you'll know at a glance if you're running out of anything.

Helpful items to keep in your kit:

Envelopes of varied size and color

Blank writing paper

Blank note cards or greeting cards for any occasion

Postcards

Invitations

Seasonal/holiday/birthday cards

Address book

Pens and pencils

Postage stamps

Address labels

organization options

You can use one of these organization options for your stationery kit or combine the two. Choose the best option or create your own system that works well with your daily life.

- **By Type:** Separate by the types listed above or come up with your own system that applies to what you have at home. To save space, get rid of individual boxes and instead tie sets together with ribbons or rubber bands.

- **By Occasion:** Keep a small calendar with your stationery kit and mark relevant special occasions, birthdays, and holidays in your calendar. If you're using an accordion file, clip a piece of paper to each section with important dates and birthdays.

smart and thrifty ideas

Decorative paper and greeting cards can be very expensive, especially when you're forced to grab something at the last minute. Try some of these tips for making the most of your stationery and finding great deals.

- **Repurpose:** Create a special section for cards, notes, or stationery you have been given that you'd like to repurpose as gift tags or use for scrapbooking purposes. You can also keep a collection of old envelopes and use the backs to write notes, take phone messages, or make a quick to-do list. Staple the envelopes at the top of a small stack to create an instant pad of recycled paper.

- **Bargain Shopping:** Keep an eye out for bargains when you're out and about or doing your regular shopping. Instead of purchasing expensive individual cards, look for blank cards and stationery that you can personalize for any occasion. You can also often find discontinued or discounted stationery and card sets seasonally that you can keep on hand for future use. With a little smart shopping, you'll have a stationery stockpile.

organized and inspirational sparkbook

There are so many things that we experience, read, or hear about in our daily lives that "spark" our inspiration. We make promises to ourselves to remember these little details, but as we get busy, it is easy to move on and forget, even with the best of intentions. What if you had a useful planning tool as your designated place to store and organize all those inspirational moments?

A Sparkbook is different from your typical planner because it not only helps you determine all the things you want to do, but it also helps you visualize them.

By collecting sketches, magazine cutouts, photographs, and bits of memorabilia from daily life along with key words, phrases, and poetry, you can create a great reference for inspiration and empowerment.

choose your book

To make your own Sparkbook, designate a blank notebook or binder you already have. Choose something that you know you'll enjoy using and fits with your personal organization preferences. Here are a few great examples of books to use:

Three-ring binder with blank or lined paper

Small photo book (without the protective sheet covers)

Scrapbook (4" × 6" or 12" × 14")

Sketchpad

Notebook

decorate it

Cover your chosen book with fabric, decorative paper, or a collage of images. The possibilities are endless.

Use scrapbooking paper to create your own label for the front cover of your Sparkbook and attach it with a glue stick. Write anything you like on your label—the year, your name, or an inspiring phrase.

organize it

Next, you'll want to figure out how to organize your book. Adding tabs, available at your local office supply store, is an easy and clear way to keep your ideas, inspirations, and plans in their own special categories.

Here are a few suggestions for possible tabbed sections, but feel free to add ones that are important and helpful to you:

- **Home Goals:** home décor and organization projects you'd like to accomplish

- **Cooking/Entertaining:** recipes and dinner party ideas you want to remember

- **Family:** activities and goals you'd like to achieve with your family

- **Personal/Wellness Goals:** your health, spirit, and personal thoughts

- **Financial Goals:** saving, budgeting, and planning

- **Travel/R&R:** places you'd like to visit in the next twelve months

- **Career:** goals, plans, and personal encouragement related to work

> **As you come across inspirational and empowering sparks in your life, insert them in your Sparkbook as you see fit. Keep your journal handy, like on a bedside table, so you can review and add to it throughout the year.**

create your own tabs

You can use these ideas as easy inspiration for creating your own tabs if your book doesn't already have them:

- Cut out swatches of fabric you enjoy and glue them to the sides of your pages. Write your section names on the swatches with a fabric marker.

- Use color-coded rubber bands: Section off and wrap rubber bands around each category.

- Insert binder dividers with tabs to create sections.

- Use colorful sticky notes and write section names on a different color for each category.

- Create your own bookmarks using ribbon, and color-code each section for easy reference.

fabric tabs

Use our simple instructions to create your own fabric tabs for your Sparkbook.

Materials

Scissors
Rectangles of fabric (4" × 1¼")
Spray starch—heavy
Warm iron

Glue stick or double-sided tape
Construction or scrapbooking paper
Permanent marker or fabric marker

Instructions

1. Cut enough fabric tabs (4" × 1¼" size) as needed for the categories you will have in your Sparkbook.

2. Fold each rectangle perfectly in half to create the finished size of 2" × 1¼".

3. To make the fabric sturdier, spray the folded rectangle with heavy starch and press with a warm iron.

4. With your glue stick or double-sided tape, stick the insides of the rectangles together, leaving the last ¼" of fabric unglued. This will be the portion of the fabric that attaches to your book pages.

5. Use a permanent marker to write the category headings on construction or scrapbooking paper that has been cut into pieces small enough to be glued to swatches to achieve the look as pictured, or you can write the category headings directly on fabric with a fabric marker.

6. Determine how many pages will be designed for each section, and which pages will become tabbed dividers. (It is easiest to have the tabbed pages made up of 3 sheets glued together, with the center sheet being the one the tab is attached to.)

7. Use a glue stick to apply glue to the remaining ¼" inside the fabric tab. Attach to the edge of the middle sheet of the three pages that will be glued together to make your "section-heading page."

8. Once the tab dries, glue the back of the first three pages you've designated to the center sheet (which is now tabbed). Then apply glue to the front of the third sheet you've designated to the tabbed sheet as well. This will give you a sturdy "section heading page" and will create a little more division between sections.

9. Follow the same process for each tab, moving the tabs down the right side of your book, alternating colors as you go.

add heading pages

Now that your tabs are in order, you can personalize your heading pages. Heading pages can be as simple as writing the name of the section at the top of the page or as creative as adding imagery and phrases that will inspire you to fill up the pages of each section.

fill in inspiration pages

To add to the inspiration pages, draw pictures or cut out words and imagery from magazines that speak to you. Add personal photographs and bits of memorabilia from your daily life and combine with key words or poetry to reference.

organize a busy bathroom

The bathroom can be an extra-busy space in the home, especially if you find yourself with too much stuff and not enough storage. Since it is the place where your family members start and end their day, try making the bathroom the most comfortable and functional place it can be. Using helpful organization ideas, you can customize your space.

Whether your bathroom is large, small, or in between, these tips will help you organize various bathroom necessities in an attractive and useful way:

organization for large bathrooms

- Place a bookshelf in your bathroom to allow extra room for mixing decorative bath items with everyday useful items.

- Tip a wooden ladder against a bathroom wall and attach it with brackets. Add wider pieces of wood to the steps for additional shelf space or for displaying decorative items.

- A travel chest or trunk can be a wonderful accent piece and a very useful place to store spare towels or linens.

- If your space allows it, consider incorporating a cushioned bench with storage inside for added comfort and space.

- Repurpose a nightstand with drawers for additional storage space. Assign a drawer to family members so they can easily store their bathroom-related belongings. You can dress up the drawers by adding personalized monograms or a picture of each person.

organization for small bathrooms

- Create one basket that contains all the items you use every day. It can be stored in a linen closet or under the sink for easy access. Create one for each family member and personalize it to their liking.

- Hang a mirror on the back of the bathroom door or the inside of the medicine cabinet to create an additional viewing space if more than one person is in the bathroom at a time.

- Over-the-commode shelving is a great space saver, and beautiful, inexpensive shelving options are widely available for purchase.

- For a pedestal sink with no cabinetry, attach a strip or hook and loop tape to the underside of the sink. Affix the matching piece of tape to a piece of fabric chosen to accent your décor and cut to size. Fabric will create the look of a skirt around the sink and provide space to have baskets for cleaning supplies, extra rolls of toilet paper, or a small trash can.

organization for all bathrooms

- Use apothecary or similar glass jars to store cotton products. It is a decorative and less cumbersome solution that lets you know when you're getting low on supplies. Your guests will also know exactly where to find these items.

- Organize towels by color, size, and type. If you are crunched for space, try storing seldom-used towels (like beach towels) in a guest room closet or on a shelf in the mudroom.

- If you have an especially busy bathroom, create a family bathroom schedule so that everyone can use the bathroom in (relative) harmony.

make the most of personal care products

When you organize or clean your bathroom, take some time to go through your products thoroughly. All products have a limited shelf life. Once this period of time is up, they may not work properly but, more important, can become contaminated. To avoid complications, follow these tips to make sure that what you are storing and using is safe:

- **General Rule:** All makeup and hair products should be used within three years of leaving the factory. Normally, the back of the product is labeled with a coded date. Or you can label your products using a permanent marker when you purchase them. Label directly on the back of the bottle or container so that you can easily tell when it is time to toss.

- **Natural or Organic Products:** These typically have a shorter life because they do not contain preservatives. Try using these products within two to three months.

- **Makeup Brushes:** Keep them clean by periodically washing in warm, soapy water. Let air-dry on a towel, and they will fluff up like new!

- **Keeping It Cool:** All makeup, hair products, and medicines should be stored in a cool, dry, dark place, away from sunlight, humidity, and heat. Try using colored, dark plastic bins or decorative baskets that keep direct sunlight from affecting the bottles.

> Remember, cleaning as you go is the key to keeping your bathroom clean and tidy. Always put your bathroom items back where they came from after each use and encourage your family to do the same.

bathroom cleaning tips

Try these tips for keeping your bathroom fresh and organized:

- Keep a bath caddy under the sink that holds Mr. Clean products and other items you need to clean your bathroom. That way everything is close at hand, and it's easy to do a quick touch-up for unexpected guests.

- As a general rule, start at the top and work your way down; for example, start with the shower walls and work down to the tub.

- The sink should be the very last thing that is cleaned because you will use it throughout the cleaning process.

- If you have a small space and no place to keep a bath caddy, consider a caddy placed in a larger closet or pantry that contains all the products you use to clean the entire house. To keep cleaning tools separate, use only one color of sponge for the bathroom and label gloves for the bathroom with the letter b.

- Febreze is the perfect finishing touch. The wonderful fresh scent really says "clean." Since Febreze comes in many scents and product styles, try a different one in each bathroom.

use an old dresser to organize

The garage, basement, and storage areas all over the home can easily become overwhelmed with cardboard boxes, tools, and more. Luckily, organizing all this stuff doesn't require expensive storage solutions. You can easily make an old dresser functional again by using it for storage. Try these inspiring ideas for making a common furniture piece useful once more.

find a dresser

If you don't have an old dresser at home that you can repurpose for storage, there are plenty of outlets for finding one. Check the classified listings in the newspaper and online or visit garage sales for great deals. You may also find inexpensive dressers at secondhand stores or flea markets. Don't worry about how it looks because you're going to give it a makeover.

spruce it up

Make sure it is functioning correctly, and then give your old dresser a new look by adding a fresh coat of paint. Tighten the drawer pulls or add new ones. Just because the dresser will be in your garage, basement, or out-of-the-way space doesn't mean it can't look great. You can paint it in one neutral color or get creative with bright colors, stripes, or designs.

Use these tips as your guide for painting wood furniture and fixing drawer pulls:

1. Wipe down the dresser inside and out to start with clean surfaces.

2. Sand until smooth with fine-grit sandpaper. Brush off excess sanding residues.

3. Apply a coat of primer (white or gray) and let dry for one to two hours. Add another coat if necessary. Gently scrape the surface with a 3-inch putty blade to easily remove small bumps that may show up after the primer has dried.

4. Add a coat of water-based paint in even strokes, following the wood grain. Allow the first coat to dry and then apply a second coat if needed. At this point you can add different colors, stripes, or designs. For easy organization you can color-code the drawers.

Make cleaning your dresser a snap by using a Swiffer to remove dust from the dresser before sanding and to brush away excess sanding residue before you start painting.

update drawer pulls

To make your drawer pulls look and work better, remove and shine them with steel wool if they're metal, or you can repaint them using a fun color of your choice. When you put the pulls back on, use new screws and tighten them. To replace with new pulls, measure the width of the current pulls before heading out to your local home improvement store.

organization ideas

Once your dresser is updated and ready to use, you'll need to decide what to organize and how to do it. Try to designate each drawer for only one category of supplies or items and use some of these tips as your starting point:

- **Seasonal Décor:** Use each drawer to store your seasonal decorations safely and so they are easy to find each year. Use a different drawer for each season or holiday.

- **Outdoor Items:** If there are large drawers, use the dresser in the garage to store outdoor toys and sporting equipment such as bats, balls, gloves, helmets, and safety pads. Organize the drawers by family member so that each person knows where to look for his or her toys and equipment.

- **Household Supplies:** Try using the drawers to organize common household needs such as cords, lightbulbs, batteries, and craft supplies. To keep your cords from turning into a tangled mess, roll them up and secure with rubber bands or twist ties. Separate different types of cords by creating dividers with cardboard.

- **Tools and Hardware:** Sort out tools, loose or miscellaneous hardware, and home repair or gardening materials. Store the tools you use most often in the top drawer and the items you need infrequently in the bottom drawer.

how-to: **organize**

- **Container Storage:** Try repurposing items you already have around the home to create individual storage compartments for loose items within drawers. Utilize desk drawer or silverware organizers to create several organized compartments. For larger pieces use shoeboxes or plastic tubs to create bins for storing.

- **Tennis Ball Storage:** If you want to collect small hardware items or odds and ends like screws, nails, hooks, and paper clips, try this unique tennis ball storage idea:

  1. Using a utility knife, cut a small slit in one side of a tennis ball, squeeze the ball to expand the slit, and drop your small items inside.

  2. Easily organize your new storage solution inside the dresser however you like. Here are a few suggestions: Use a permanent marker or sticker labels to designate what is inside each tennis ball. Place the tennis balls inside a box or bin to keep them from rolling around.

> After you have decided how to organize, add labels to the outside of the drawers so that the items can be found easily. Get creative by attaching custom labels or painting directly on the drawers.

baskets to the rescue

Give your home the treatment it deserves by encouraging your family to work together to keep it clutter-free. A personalized storage basket for each family member is a simple and effective way for families of all sizes and ages to eliminate the piling up of belongings throughout the home. Organized baskets look much nicer—and function much better—than piles heaped on countertops, tables, and stairways. Plus, it will help build a sense of responsibility in each family member for keeping your home clean and tidy.

> Achieve an antique, artistic feel with ease by converting your photos to black and white or sepia tone on your computer before you print.

getting started on personalized storage baskets

1. Attractive wicker storage baskets with washable cotton liners are available at most home décor stores. Consider using a different colored liner for each family member's basket so they can be easily identified.

2. Next, personalize the baskets for each family member by attaching a fun photo or image to each basket. Use safety pins or clothespins so that you can change the photos easily as the children grow or you find a new favorite photo to use.

3. Make sure your baskets are large enough to hold an ample amount of personal belongings—the type that tend to pile up around the house. Be careful not to make them so large that they become "catch-all" containers that are cumbersome to carry and difficult to store.

putting your baskets to use

Each storage basket should be a personal "inbox" where you can distribute mail or place CDs, DVDs, notebooks, cell phones, hair accessories, and other personal items that frequently get left lying around the house.

If you have little ones, teach them to use their storage baskets to collect toys and other items that need to be put away. For older kids, suggest they use the baskets to transport school supplies and papers to where they belong.

Use your creativity and fun to encourage your family to use the storage baskets as part of their daily routines. For example, start a contest where the family member who does the best job of using his or her storage basket to pick up personal belongings throughout the week gets to: decide what's for breakfast on Saturday or Sunday morning; choose the movie for family movie night; select a special treat from the grocery or bakery to share with the entire family.

> Associating different baskets with specific items is a smart and simple way to teach young ones basic organizational skills. Consider labeling the front with an image of the basket's contents.

keep the baskets handy

For your family's new storage baskets to work effectively, they need to be kept in areas that are out of the way and yet easily accessible. You can keep them all in one spot or in convenient areas for each member. Here are a few examples of good locations for keeping baskets:

- **For Smaller Children:** a corner of a playroom or family room

- **For Teenagers:** near their desk or at the foot of their bed

- **For You:** in the kitchen or near your work space

Another possible solution is to find a convenient place to store everyone's baskets in the same high-traffic area for easy access, such as: under a bench in the entryway; going up the stairs, with one basket per stair placed out of the way on the far left or right; or on a shelf in the utility room or hall closet close to the kitchen.

Wherever you decide, make sure all family members agree on the best location for their baskets when you first begin using them. Also ask your family to keep them in the same location so you'll know exactly where they are when you want to place wayward belongings in their baskets.

helpful hooks

Hooks are small and unassuming, but when it comes to getting a lot of organization out of a little, they really hold their own—and they're inexpensive, too! Maximize your wall space storage with this tiny piece of wonderful hardware.

five kinds

Hooks come in all shapes, sizes, and forms. You can choose from a variety of beautiful options at your local hardware or home store, or you can transform unexpected objects into hooks yourself. Here are some ideas to get you started finding the stylish solution for you.

1. **Vintage Curtain Tiebacks:** There aren't many people using ornate curtain tiebacks anymore, but that doesn't mean they don't still have a very functional use. Look for some online or at your local antique store. They are easy to repurpose because they were made to mount on a wall. All you might have to do is pick up a new screw or two at the hardware store if the originals are missing. Then mount and hang! Try them as beautiful decorative coat hooks in your entryway or anywhere you want to make a statement while you store.

2. **Drawer Pulls:** Unique drawer pulls are also simple and fun. Look for interesting drawer pulls at home décor stores. Many are adorned with beads or painted patterns. Choose several of the same style or mix and match to create an eclectic focal point. Use them for hanging smaller, more delicate items.

3. **Doorknobs:** These are more likely to be found at a thrift shop or antique store. Worn brass knobs tell the story of a well-loved home. Ornate glass knobs remind you of a period gone by. Line them up anywhere you see fit. Because of their large round shape, they are better for holding hats and scarves than a traditional hook.

4. **Kitchen Utensils:** Put your forks and spoons to work in a new way. In a few steps you can turn an old utensil into a hook for your apron,

towel, or pot holder. All you need is an old fork, two medium-sized nails, and a hammer.

First, hammer the nail where you want the fork to go. Next, turn the fork upside down and slide it against the wall so that the nail is wedged between two of the tines. Finally, hammer the second nail between the other tines. Now you're ready to hang your favorite kitchen items on the fork handle.

5. **Knotty Driftwood:** Driftwood is both naturally beautiful and easy to use as a rack. The key is choosing a piece with the knots and twists you need. Take a walk by a nearby river and look for a piece of driftwood that has at least two knots or bumps that can be used as hooks. At home, secure it to the wall using two long screws, preferably spaced so that each is in a wall stud.

> For a more contemporary look, paint your driftwood with white spray paint or interior wall paint that complements your wall color.

five uses

1. **Accessories:** Keep accessories like necklaces, bracelets, scarves, and headbands tangle-free with drawer pull hooks. Hang them where they can be admired—by your vanity, for instance—or tuck them away in a bedroom or bathroom closet.

2. **Outfits:** Not needing to think each morning about pulling together your day's look can be a real timesaver. Organize the week's outfits ahead of time and hang them on separate hooks so you can grab and go from Monday through Friday. You may even be able to sleep in a few minutes longer!

3. **Kitchen Gadgets:** Keep often-used items within reach, such as measuring spoons, dish towels, and pot holders. Try a hook beside the sink for towels or above the counter of your favorite work space for measuring spoons.

4. **Play Clothes:** Dress-ups get wrinkly in a chest and often end up on the floor after playtime. Try hanging dress-up clothes within little arms' reach to make them easily accessible and even easier to put away.

5. **Frames:** Photo frame hooks don't have to be hidden. First, glue or nail a piece of ribbon to the two uppermost corners on the back of the frame. Make sure the ribbon is long enough to make room for

the hook it will hang on. For a medium photo frame or mirror, try using a doorknob or a vintage curtain tieback as a hook. For smaller items, try eye-catching drawer pulls.

five places

1. **Bedroom Door:** Keep often-used clothing, like pajamas and sweatshirts, out of sight and off the floor by making a place for them on the back side of each family member's bedroom door.

2. **Utility Room:** Give all family members their own hook in a community space, such as the utility room, for coats and backpacks.

3. **Coat Closets:** Try the side and back walls of coat closets for extra accessories like umbrellas and reusable grocery bags. They are often easier to find on a hook than buried in a basket.

4. **Bathroom:** In a busy bathroom, use towel hooks instead of racks to save on space and folding time.

5. **Pet Areas:** Hang leashes, brushes, bags of toys, and other pet-related supplies together in one accessible spot.

> **Hang hooks high and low for family members of every size.**

hand-me-forwards

Sometimes it's hard to let go of items around your home even if their only value is sentimental. Your high school prom dress and your kids' baby books are just a few things you may think twice about parting with. But it is easier when you know your special things are going to someone who will make the most of them. Even if your sentimental tokens have been given away, your memories will always be with you. And when your unused items are in the hands of someone who needs them, they can help others make happy memories, too. Here are a few ideas on how to minimize the clutter and make a difference at the same time.

de-clutter

Just think: it's going to feel great to minimize the clutter chaos that can pile up around your space. The first step is identifying the items you're going to give away and gathering them up. Get some boxes ready to fill. Then start at one end of your home and work toward the other. Many organizations have wish lists of items they need most. In case you don't have one, here are some ideas of what to look for:

- **Apparel:** Go from top to bottom in your closet looking through hats, purses, tops, belts, pants, and shoes. You may like something, but if you haven't worn it at all this season or once this year, consider putting it to better use as a donation item.

- **Next Season's Clothes:** Take a few minutes to sift through your out-of-season wardrobe and streamline it so you have room for a few new pieces next season.

- **Jewelry:** Accessories are great items to donate to organizations that help women get on their feet with a new job. Something as simple as a fashion necklace from a department store could help someone get the confidence she needs to shine in an interview.

- **Furniture:** Is it collecting dust in the basement? It could furnish a proud new homeowner's space instead.

- **Boxed-up Memorabilia:** Check out the boxes stacked in your basement or attic. Do you need all the kids' toys or clothes? Maybe you can pick out a few that mean the most to you and donate the rest. How about wedding gifts that have never been used or old tableware you've since replaced? These are all wonderful contributions to an organization near you, and you get to take a nice walk down memory lane as you sort!

- **Everyday Toys:** Get your family involved by asking them to work together choosing items they don't feel your family really needs. This could include board games, electronic games, CDs or DVDs, toys, and even sports equipment like bats, balls, and old golf clubs.

family first

Now you're ready to go somewhere with your stuff. Before contacting a nonprofit organization, ask around in your circle of friends and extended family. Someone close to you may have a need you didn't know about.

- **Nieces and Nephews:** A sister or cousin may have a child just a few years younger who can wear the clothes your child has outgrown.

- **Girlfriends:** Consider trading clothes with family and friends. You could even put together an afternoon of snacking and trading clothes with friends, sisters, aunts, and cousins. After all, we all have a few items in our closet that never fit us quite right but may fit another person just perfectly!

- **College Kids:** Are your siblings college age—or maybe your own kids? See if they need furniture or kitchen appliances for their dorm or first apartment. Even if they don't, they're sure to appreciate the kind gesture.

> Many charitable organizations will schedule pickups, especially for large items. And don't forget the receipt so you can get a small tax credit. Every little bit counts!

donate

If you don't already have a favorite organization for donations, there are many places to choose from, including battered women's shelters, special needs facilities, and children's homes, to name just a few. Pick one or two in your community that have missions near and dear to you. Start by looking online and ask around to learn more about nonprofits that you aren't familiar with. It is important to know that the facility you choose is a reputable organization.

work space

Keep a handy list of your favorite organizations here.

Organization	Contact Name	Phone #

gift-wrap storage solution

With all the holiday celebrations and gift-giving occasions, wouldn't it be wonderful to have all your gift-wrapping supplies right at your fingertips? With a simple clothing hamper you can make it happen! Just follow our easy directions to create your own holiday supplies storage hamper that will be a useful gift-giving and time-saving tool for years to come.

holiday supplies storage hamper

We all have our own short-term solutions for storing gift wrap and wrapping accessories such as bows and tags. Even with the best storage intentions, wrapping can be a challenge to keep organized. Many times the necessary supplies end up scattered in various places around the home and aren't right there when you need them.

If you follow these step-by-step instructions for creating a holiday supplies storage hamper, your wrapping paper, bows, tags, ribbon, and more can go wherever you need them and be in one portable and organized container.

1. Purchase a plastic or woven wicker hamper with handles and a removable lid. It should be tall enough to hold tubes of wrapping paper upright, but still allow you to close the lid.

2. Attach hooks through holes in the wicker weave or at the top of the hamper for hanging various supplies. Here are a few options for using your hooks:

   - Keep gift bags close at hand and looking great by hanging them from their handles on the hooks.

   - Use hooks to hang a bag with handles to hold bows, ribbon, and tags.

   - Hang a bag that will hold your holiday cards and a list of recipients or an address book.

> If you choose a woven wicker hamper, look for one that Is lined with fabric to protect your supplies from tearing.

- Use a pencil case with three-ring binder holes to hold your scissors, tape, pens, or any other small wrapping accessories. Include a few pens in festive colors to add a special finishing touch to cards and tags. Hang from a hook through a binder hole.

- Or try our easy, no-sew felt pocket (see page 52) for storing small wrapping accessories.

3. Fill your hamper with various tubes of gift wrap, tissue paper, and a few flattened gift boxes in various sizes. Use fabric or sturdy plastic drawstring bags to hold boxes and tissue paper in their own separate compartments. This way you won't have to dig through the hamper to find the supplies you are looking for. Simply grab the bag with the items you need.

4. Keep the hamper light so that you can take it wherever it's needed. Set up your portable gift-wrapping station near your dining room table, in a rec room, or in the family room. Look for areas with large spaces and flat surfaces so you can spread out.

5. Store the hamper in an easily accessible yet out-of-the-way place when not in use. Good storage options might be a linen closet, underneath a basement staircase, or in a corner of your laundry room.

after the holidays

After the holidays are over, keep these ideas in mind to help make your holiday supplies storage hamper work for you all year round.

- **Personalize your greetings.** Holidays are a great opportunity to catch up with friends and family and show you care. Keep all those cards you received from loved ones last year in a gift bag or felt pocket on your storage hamper for easy reference. Also, keep a notepad in the bag to jot down events and accomplishments throughout the year that you know you'll want to share when it's time to send out your holiday greetings. We all know how easy it is to forget things during the hectic holidays!

- **Stock up to save time and money.** Another way to save time and a good deal of money is to stock up on your wrapping paper, rib-

bon, bows, cards, gift bags, and boxes right after the holidays when retailers offer huge discounts. Also look for sales throughout the year on things such as tape and stationery. Buy all you'll need for the coming holiday season and store it in your hamper. It will be there when you need it during the busiest of seasons.

no-sew felt pocket

Materials

Scissors

Felt in a festive color (9" × 12" if it is precut)

Permanent marker

Ruler

Heavy-duty hole punch

Spool of ¼-inch ribbon

Instructions

1. Use the scissors to cut a 9" × 12" rectangle of felt.

2. Lay the felt flat on a table and use a permanent marker to lightly mark dots ½ inch from the edge and ½ inch apart on each side. Use the ruler to keep the dots lined up. (Leave approximately 1 inch in the center of each edge without dots; this is where the felt will be folded in half.)

3. Keep the felt flat and use your hole punch to create holes along two sides of the rectangle where you made your dots.

4. Fold the felt in half, leaving an opening at the top.

5. Thread the ribbon through the holes, tying a knot or bow at the bottom on each side.

6. Tie the top ends of the ribbon to the hamper through the wicker holes or onto a handle or hook. (Feel free to experiment with how you tie the ribbon.)

color made simple

Choosing color combinations for a room can be one of the most difficult decisions in redecorating. With so many beautiful colors, so many patterns, and so many ways to mix and match, it is easy to feel as if there is no good place to start. But there is a solution: Learn about the color wheel, every designer's secret to creating sophisticated spaces. It is a timeless tool that you can reference again and again to select the perfect palette for any room in your home.

Many professional designers rely on the color wheel for ideas and inspiration because it helps them understand and better predict how colors will interact. Before you make big purchases that aren't easily reversed—such as furniture, fabrics, and paint—turn to the color wheel to be sure of your decisions. Then keep it on hand as you continue to redesign your room. You can also use it to select artwork, photographs, accent décor, and more.

color wheel fundamentals

The color wheel is comprised of three types of colors: primary, secondary, and tertiary.

Primary Colors are the foundation for all other colors:

Red
Blue
Yellow

Secondary Colors result from the marriage of two primary colors:

Violet (red and blue)
Green (blue and yellow)
Orange (yellow and red)

Tertiary Colors represent the mixture of a primary color and a secondary color:

Blue-violet
Red-violet
Red-orange

Yellow-orange
Yellow-green
Blue-green

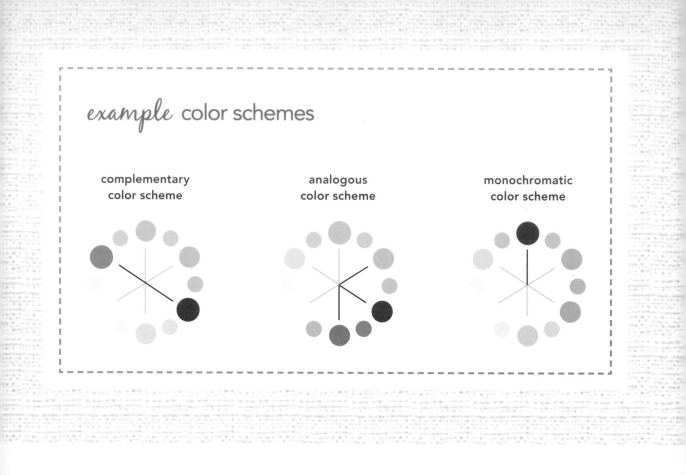

example color schemes

complementary color scheme

analogous color scheme

monochromatic color scheme

pick a dominant color

Every color scheme begins with a dominant color. At least half of your room should feature this hue, so think of it as the anchor of your overall design. Pick a color—any color—and then let it guide your additional color choices, using the static placement of colors within the wheel to quickly and easily create any number of stunning schemes.

classic: complementary color scheme

For more formal spaces, such as dining rooms, a complementary color scheme is perfect for achieving a classic look. To create one, find your dominant color's complementary color, the one that sits directly opposite it on the wheel. Beautiful combinations include blue and orange and yellow and violet. Think of your complementary color as playing a supporting role to the dominant color. Let it shine through in window treat-

ments, furniture upholstery, and rugs. To add a final layer of color to a complementary scheme, select an accent color to feature in smaller décor accessories, from pillows to pottery. Choose the color directly to the left or right of your complementary color on the wheel—for example, a predominantly red room with complementary green features and yellow accents makes for a gorgeous palette.

> Beware of going too rich: Using deep, dark versions of each of your colors can make a room feel heavy and oversaturated. Explore mixing darker and lighter hues instead.

casual: analogous color scheme

This approach, which uses adjacent colors on the wheel, is often recommended for more casual spaces, such as bedrooms and rec rooms. Pick a dominant color and then use the two colors to the left or right as the supporting and accent colors. You can also create a scheme with one color to the left and one color to the right of your dominant color—a red, violet, and blue scheme is an inspired example. As you choose your hues, make sure you have enough contrast between colors. If you want to add more depth, try throwing in occasional splashes of black and white to make your palette pop.

modern: monochromatic color scheme

Achieving a monochromatic look involves playing with different tints (color plus white) and shades (color plus black) of your dominant color. Envision a room in shades and tints of orange, from tangerine to pumpkin, or completely in blue, transitioning from steely gray to peacock blue to dark navy. Like the analogous scheme, it is important to create enough contrast for a nice range of color. Simplify the monochromatic scheme by picking three tints or shades of a color and then use one as dominant, one as supporting, and one as your accent.

work space

Using the color wheel, make note of the palettes you'd like to try in specific rooms of your home.

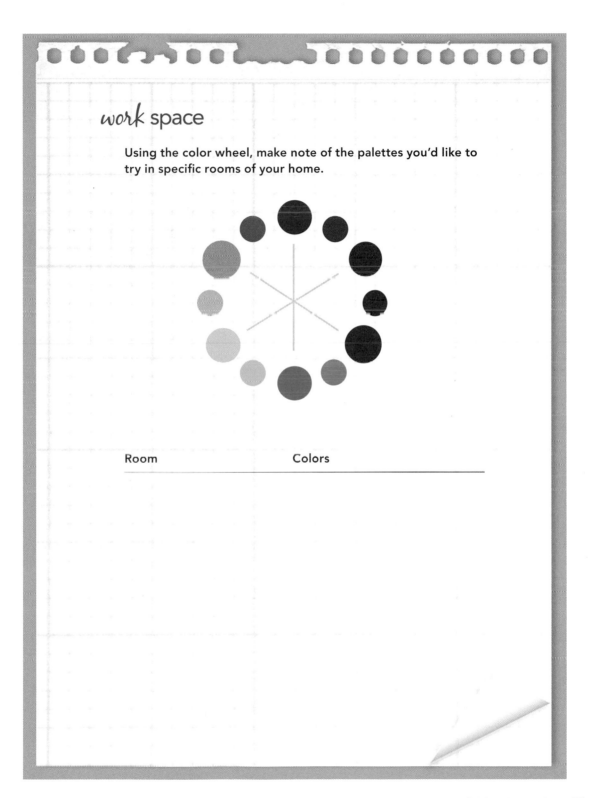

Room   Colors

celebrate living

welcome. appreciate. *celebrate.*

Opening your home and sharing your life with special people can create some of your most treasured moments. Even though our day-to-day lives are busy, it's important to take time to celebrate the milestones that make life memorable.

Entertaining has a different meaning for each of us. For some it is a chance to show kindness and creativity. For others it is an opportunity to share a passion for cooking. Or it may simply be about spending quality time with the ones we love.

There is always a good reason to welcome your favorite people into your home or show your appreciation with a sweet, simple gift. Whether it is a handmade present, dinner party tips, or holiday celebration ideas, we will help you dazzle your family and friends in beautiful, budget-friendly ways. You will be ready to entertain to your heart's content any time of year.

the basics of entertaining

Every get-together has its own style, and every hostess is unique. Do you love throwing quick and casual barbecues? Or maybe you're more about formal four-course feasts. No matter how much of your fabulous personality you put into your parties, adhering to a few fundamentals will help you plan something that will certainly be remembered. Here are a few of them to refer to the next time you are planning your next event.

brunch boundaries

A breezy brunch is a great way to create late-morning sociability. You will be able to present breakfast and your home in their best light by sticking to these timeless tips:

- **Stick to the classics.** For a brunch that never misses the mark, serve plenty of coffee, juice, muffins, and an assortment of seasonal fruit. For heartier fare, throw together a quick egg or cheesy potato casserole, which usually appeals to a wide variety of tastes and diets.

- **Incorporate some fruit flair.** If you want to show off some originality, have fun with the choice of drinks. Consider flavorful spritzers, unique "mocktails," or surprisingly delightful pitchers of pretty punch.

- **Work less and have more fun.** To keep from missing the fun altogether, shy away from dishes that require any last-minute work beyond a super-fast reheat or two. This includes absolutely no hovering over the stove to scramble eggs, flip flapjacks, or create complicated made-to-order omelets.

- **Garnish simply.** Let the natural beauty of fresh flowers say all your "good mornings" and "welcomes." Buy a few of your favorite blooms and decorate simply with some small store-bought or homemade bud vases. These sweet creations could be given away later as party favors.

cocktail hour

Nothing is more festive and lighthearted than an evening cocktail party with plenty of small, delicious, quick bites. Keep these suggestions in mind when you're planning the big night:

- **Calculate Carefully:** A cocktail party usually centers on refreshment, so make sure you buy enough for everyone to drink. Whatever is on tap, a good general rule is to account for three drinks per person for an average-sized party. Roughly estimated, that's about 36 ounces of beverage, and about half a pound of ice per person.

- **Food, Too:** An assortment of hot and cold small plates gives you the perfect opportunity to show off your secret (or not-so-secret) culinary creativity. Many caterers follow the rules and assign a minimum of twelve appetizers (total) per person. For about ten guests, three types of small snacks will do. Up to four different appetizers will be plenty for between ten and twenty guests. Around six is good for between twenty and fifty people, but plan to have a spread of at least eight different appetizers for a guest list larger than fifty.

- **Party Tunes:** As your party gets into full swing, the sounds of conversation and laughter will fill the air, of course. To make sure the atmosphere stays as casual and as relaxed as possible, layer music into the background. Collect and play an eclectic assortment of crowd favorites; put the mix on shuffle so that you don't have to be a DJ the whole night. If the guests are all getting to know one another for the first time, play it safe with a sound track chock-full of snappy jazz, reggae, pop, or classic standards.

sit-down dinner party parameters

Since a dinner party usually has more structure and formality, an event of this type may require a bit more preplanning. And since no hostess ever wants anyone to leave hungry, the big question concerning these kinds of gatherings always seems to be: "Exactly how much food should I make?" Use these tips as benchmarks for finding the perfect amount.

- **Think Ahead:** Many entertaining experts agree that thinking about a menu six weeks in advance gives you plenty of time to gather ingredients, create a cooking game plan, and keep yourself from completely stressing out on the days leading up to the gathering.

- **Filler Up:** Make plenty of "filler" foods available, whether served as the first course or placed in small bowls on end tables. These foods, such as bread, nuts, and olives, will instantly fill any "hungry moments."

- **Cooking Criteria:** If you are serving chicken or turkey breasts, plan to buy about ½ to ¾ pound per person. Pork dishes usually require the same amount or maybe a little less. Fish or steaks run about a ¼ to ½ pound per person. Along with any appetizers, also plan on serving two to three sides and two or three desserts, depending on the number of guests at the table.

perfectly placed

A properly set table is the canvas for a beautiful meal, so use this cheat sheet the next time you want to set the stage for something amazing.

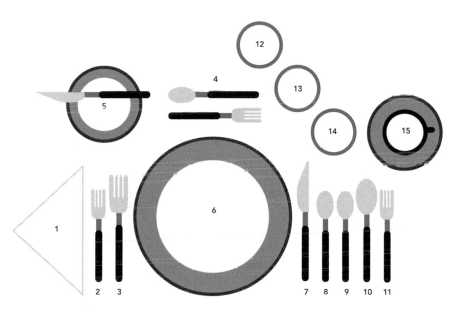

1. Napkin
2. Salad fork
3. Dinner fork
4. Dessert fork and coffee spoon
5. Bread and butter plate with spreader
6. Dinner plate
7. Dinner knife
8. Teaspoon
9. Teaspoon
10. Soup spoon
11. Cocktail fork
12. Water glass
13. Red wine glass
14. White wine glass
15. Coffee cup and saucer

tips to simplify everyday life

Every day you spend a few minutes here and there on small tasks—and before you know it, the little details that keep home, job, and family running smoothly have eaten up the hours. Take back the day with a few tried-and-true tips that help simplify things, leaving you more time to spend with the ones who make it all worthwhile.

entertaining and gift giving

- **Entertain at home.** Invite neighbors and friends to your home for dinner or brunch. This will keep you at home with the kids instead of out at a restaurant—and will help create many memories for you and your children.

- **Start a new tradition.** After a long workweek, everyone is beat, so why not officially deem Friday night as your weekly pizza night? Expand the new tradition and invite neighbors. Put on a fun movie for the kids and set up a card game for the adults. Time spent with friends, zero cooking, and minimal cleanup—what could be better?

- **Keep a stock of gifts.** Set aside time a few times a year to purchase gifts for the children in your life. Make a note of upcoming birthdays and remember your friends who are expecting, then buy presents accordingly.

- **Save delivery boxes.** The next time you get something delivered to your home, be sure to save the box if it is a good size and in decent condition. This allows you to box up a gift at home instead of at the post office, saving you lots of time and money.

- **Use gift bags.** The next time you are giving a gift, forgo the wrapping paper and opt for a bag. They come in a variety of sizes and styles, and they can be reused by the recipient, all the while saving lots of time. When receiving presents, be sure to save bags and repurpose them for future gifts.

general tips and time-savers

- **Never take the stairs empty-handed.** When you find something that needs to go upstairs, place it at the bottom of the stairs, and vice versa for items that need to go downstairs. When you go up or down the stairs, remember to grab the pile and put each item back in its respective place. Make this idea even easier and decorative with our personalized family storage baskets on page 39.

- **Stretch Sunday night cooking.** Each Sunday night as you prepare dinner, try to cook at least one additional meal. This will reduce your burden during the workweek so you can spend more time before and after dinner with the family.

- **Limit your child's activities.** Making your kids happy is important, but promising too much can instill unrealistic expectations in children. Let them participate in one or two sports or lessons per season and check with them regularly to make sure they are not feeling overwhelmed.

- **Take all-inclusive vacations.** Vacations can take a lot of time to plan. Simplify the process by choosing an all-inclusive travel package. Airfare, transportation, meals, and entertainment are often all included, making it perfect for a family seeking adventure and relaxation.

> **Try an idea called the "80/20 rule." Set aside the 80 percent of tasks that can wait and focus on the 20 percent that truly matter.**

inexpensive ideas, beautiful results

Dinner parties are a fun way to entertain friends and family. When planning a lovely evening with friends, you may feel overwhelmed by the details to be worked out and the expense. With a little imagination and some creative and inexpensive ideas, you can have a beautiful dinner on a budget.

before the party

Leading up to the party, you'll want to take care of a few tasks that will make the night go smoothly and be more fun for you and your guests. Will your party be a casual get-together or a fancy affair? What kind of food will you serve? The theme of the night is up to you, but advance planning makes it easier to accomplish imaginative ideas while staying within your budget.

invitations

Ask your friends to your dinner party in style with these economical invitations that mimic the look of fancy place cards:

1. Start with a set of inexpensive plain white or cream-colored 3" × 5" folded cards and envelopes.

2. Choose a spool of 1-inch velvet ribbon in a dark, rich color such as red, purple, or blue. Try to pick one that matches your look or theme.

3. Cut a piece of ribbon to fit the length of the card and glue down firmly along the bottom front edge of the card.

4. Write the guests' names nicely just above the ribbon and carefully write the party details inside the card in a matching color.

> Depending on your plan for the night, you may want to note preferred attire on your invitations. Even if your party is going to be casual, make sure to let your guests know this ahead of time so that no one is overdressed and uncomfortable.

the menu

Planning your menu ahead will give you time to look for deals on vegetables, cuts of meat, and other ingredients instead of buying at the last minute. You'll end up with better items for less and the food you really want to serve.

When shopping, also consider how you will be presenting your food and how it will look on the plate. Adding appetizing color can be as simple and inexpensive as buying red potatoes, vibrant carrots, or colorful bell peppers. For recipe ideas that are as delicious as they are beautiful, check out our Clever Kitchen section, starting on page 121.

As a low-cost added touch, print your menu, listing each course and drink selection. Use an elegant font for a formal party or a simpler font for a casual one. Place a menu next to each place setting.

food presentation

The way you present your food can make the difference between an everyday meal and a memorable dining experience. Our desire for food is driven by what we see, so a beautifully presented plate or platter will increase the elegance and the appetites of your family and friends.

- **Garnish on a Budget:** A simple and budget-friendly way to present food is to use ingredients from your dishes as garnish on the plates. Sprigs of thyme, rosemary, cilantro, or Italian parsley add color and scent to make your meal more enticing. You can also add color and flavor with a complementary garnish such as wedges or slices of lemon, lime, or orange.

- **Pretty Platters.** If you are serving food from platters, try presenting a meat entrée surrounded by colorful vegetables. Instead of tossing a salad, arrange it in layers or on a platter with the vegetables. Place rows with the brightest on the outer edge and the greens in the center.

- **Simply Impressive Dessert:** Use stemware to present a decadent-looking but simple dessert. Layer the ingredients of your choice in a glass—for example, chocolate pudding or mousse, whipped cream and raspberries or strawberries, and with coconut or chocolate shavings to top it off.

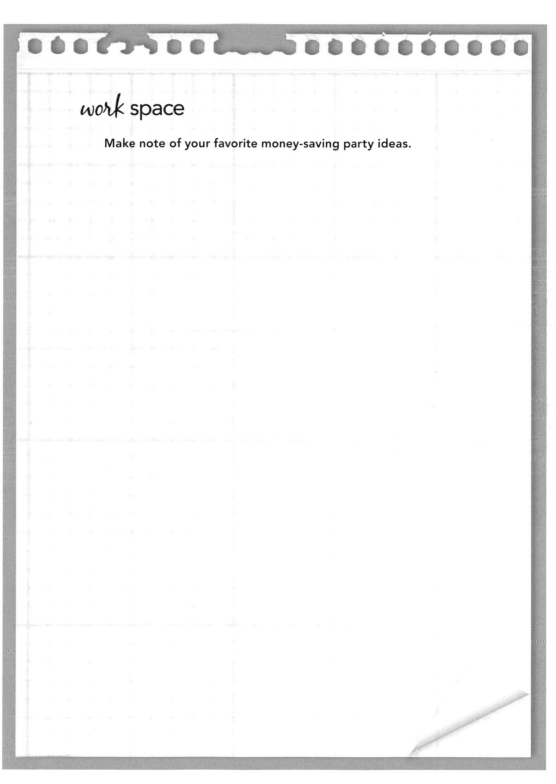

work space

Make note of your favorite money-saving party ideas.

beautiful budget décor

Creating an eye-catching table with interesting place settings and centerpieces is an excellent way to give your dinner party a fun or impressive look without spending a lot of money.

- **Centerpiece Idea:** Bring your table together by creating a natural centerpiece using bare branches you've gathered from your yard or a park. Arrange these artfully in a tall glass vase. In an instant you have an organic and inexpensive centerpiece. You can keep the branches unadorned or attach accents to fit the season or occasion. When placing a centerpiece, make sure it is not blocking your guests from seeing one another or chatting across the table.

- **Set the Mood:** Set a calm and relaxing mood by dimming the lights and placing candles tastefully around the table. Have a friend or family member light the candles just as your guests are seated.

- **Perfect Place Settings:** For an easy and distinctive look, tie a bow with simple ribbon or raffia around a knife, fork, and spoon. (Add a soup spoon or salad fork if you will be serving these dishes.) You can even fold your napkins for a finished look that costs nothing at all! Use these simple instructions (opposite) to learn how.

decorative napkin folding: the pocket

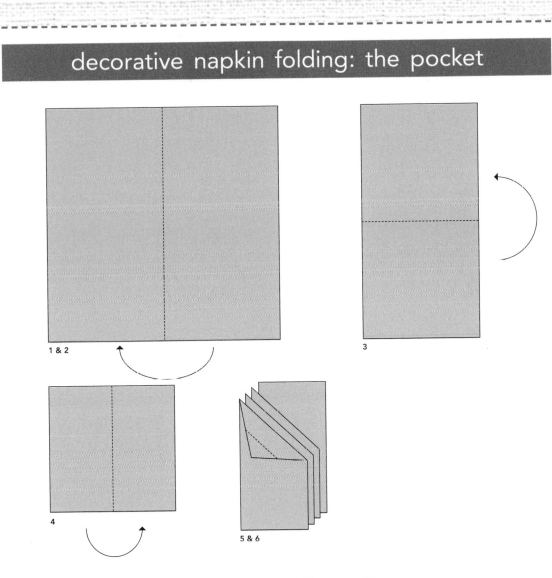

1. Start with a large square paper or linen napkin laid flat on a table.

2. Fold the napkin in half, long-ways, right to left.

3. Fold the napkin in half, bottom to top.

4. Fold in half again, left to right.

5. Make sure the loose edges of the napkin are at the top right and carefully fold each layer diagonally and under each other, leaving one large pocket in the back. You can also fold the corner of the first layer under, to create a straight line, or leave it open.

6. Place utensils in the back pocket, and a sprig of decoration in the front pocket.

one-two-three tablescapes

The table is the focus at any brunch get-together or dinner party. Setting the stage with beautiful festive table décor is easier than it looks if you know the basics. Otherwise known as tablescapes, tabletop décor can be simple but creative. Learn these fundamentals, and you can bring these fresh ideas to life or put together your own designs.

the basics

Think about your table composition as a mountain shape. Like the peak, slope, and valley of a mountainside, there are three levels to a tablescape. The centerpiece or center décor should always be the tallest, drawing the eye to the table. From the top of your centerpiece, the height of your décor should cascade down to the table level. The three main levels are centerpiece, mid level, and plate or table level.

- **Centerpiece:** This is the focal point of your table. It can be one tall item, such as a large flower arrangement, or a cluster of items, such as a set of candelabras or three vases of varying heights filled with seasonal fruits, vegetables, or submerged flowers. Whatever you choose, it should call attention to your table from afar and draw your guests in. Also make sure that your centerpiece is either low enough to see over, tall enough to see under, or thin enough to see around easily.

- **Mid Level:** The items at this level finish off the look of the centerpiece and fill the space between your place settings and platters. They are smaller than the centerpiece but sit higher than the plate level to create a flow from the visual focal point down to what matters most: the food! Here you can use objects that complement the theme you have set with your centerpiece. It is also a great place to tie the centerpiece together with your place settings by using the colors or patterns from both in the space in between.

For great ideas about favors that your guests will never forget, see Thankful Holiday Favors on page 79.

- **Table Level:** This level is the lowest area in your tablescape. It is often where you set the color palette with your linens and dishes. This is also where you add a personal touch for guests with place card holders, favors, or both. Stylish or festive napkin holders also create interest at each setting.

fall holiday

Bring the beauty of fall to your Thanksgiving table. This tablescape is an inexpensive yet elegant feast for the eyes.

- **Centerpiece:** Fill three large vases with slender tree branches. Try to choose ones that have colorful leaves. You can cut the branches from your own backyard or a nearby patch of woods. If the leaves have already fallen from the trees, use bare branches instead and simply scatter leaves at the tablecloth level.

- **Mid Level:** Place small pumpkins and gourds around the table, encircling the three large vases. Depending on the way you have created your centerpiece, they may lay on a bed of bright fall leaves.

- **Table Level:** Try simple, clean plates with shiny silverware. Add jewel-tone accents such as warm brown, rich red, or deep purple napkins. There are several ways you can treat your napkins. One idea is to use shiny silver napkin rings that match your silverware. A more casual but festive approach is to tie the napkins with raffia or twine and place a fall leaf under each knot.

To make a statement, substitute peonies for the roses, which are larger and bolder. Lisianthus comes in soft pastels and gives off a wonderful fragrance. Also consider carnations for a great look that costs less.

bridal shower

Celebrate the milestone of a friend or family member with this soft and feminine tablescape that is perfect for showers.

- **Centerpiece:** Choose a large silver vase. Fill it with white or pale pink roses. Using a single type of flower makes the process of arranging much quicker and simpler. Just toss in the flowers and place the vase.

- **Mid Level:** Try miniature vases containing one bloom each. Or alternate the mini vases with color-coordinating votives in holders of silver or coordinating colors.

- **Table Level:** Here is where your pattern comes in. Create a mix of antique or vintage china plates to create an eclectic look. Thrift shops are a great place to find single china pieces. Or to make this happen without buying different sets, ask two or three of your friends or closest guests to lend you a few of their china settings. Then mix and match. Feature handmade place cards with the guest's name and a bridal scrapbooking element glued to the place card. For a tablecloth use solid linen in antique white or ivory.

With a few tweaks this tablescape is also great for baby showers. Just adapt the flower color: blue for a boy, pink for a girl, or yellow if it's a surprise. Then give the place cards a baby theme, too.

spring has sprung

For spring entertaining get inspired by Sunday's best dresses and egg hunts. It is the perfect look for a brunch gathering.

- **Centerpiece:** Find a glass terrarium and fill it with moss. You can probably find a decorative terrarium or apothecary jar at your local home store. Next, top the moss with artificial robins' eggs and small ceramic birds. Place one green potted plant in the center.

- **Mid Level:** Position smaller potted plants around the terrarium. Use planters that coordinate with the pastel theme or whitewash some inexpensive terra-cotta pots. All you need to do is paint them with one layer of watered-down white craft paint.

- **Table Level:** Use a floral tablecloth that brings out the blues and greens in the terrarium. White plates create a bright and cheerful feel when placed on the patterned cloth beneath them. For place cards fill an artificial nest with robins' eggs and attach a small piece of paper with the name handwritten on it. To create tiny nests yourself, wind dark raffia around your finger several times. This will create the nest shape. Place an egg inside each nest, and your place cards are ready to go!

Every year we gather around the Thanksgiving table and express what we are thankful for. For most it is friends and family. This year you can create some take-home favors that not only add decorative whimsy to your table but also show your loved ones just how much you appreciate them.

a framed gesture

When it is time for everyone to sit down, guests will be touched to see simple place cards that double as take-home favors. Purchase small, inexpensive picture frames for each place setting and then insert your favorite photo of each guest. Depending on your table décor, you can print color copies to add new hues to the tablescape, or you can opt for black and white to ensure that the photos mesh well.

To add an extra personal touch, write a short note telling each person why you are thankful that he or she is in your life. You can write on the

back of the picture or on a piece of card stock glued to the back of the frame. When you set the table, place the frames in front of each person's place setting, making a point of encouraging your guests to take their heartfelt gift home.

give thanks with food

Sharing food and traditions with the people closest to you lies at the heart of the holidays. The simple act of sharing food around a table leads to laughter, storytelling, and meaningful memories, so consider passing on the experience by giving the guests a gift to take home and share at their own table.

Compile all the recipes that you served at your holiday meal and make copies of each one on note cards. Neatly stack the recipe cards and tie each bundle with a piece of decorative ribbon. Attach a festive embellishment such as a sprig of berries or a garland, if you wish. You can also thread a short thank-you note through the end of the ribbon. This way your guests can share your recipes at their own upcoming holiday celebrations and think of you each time.

> **A roll of mints or a satchel of soothing peppermint tea leaves is the perfect final offering. Use small pieces of card stock and an artistic hand to create handmade labels quickly for each treat.**

thankfully sweet pumpkin cookies

Cookies can always bring a smile to someone's face, and giving cookies is an especially sweet way to say thank you. Personalize each place setting by writing each guest's first initial on a soft, spicy pumpkin cookie with icing. Serve these as part of dessert or wrap them in colorful tissue paper as a take-home treat.

MAKES ABOUT 3 DOZEN COOKIES

Ingredients

- 1 cup granulated sugar
- 1 egg
- 1 cup shortening
- 1 teaspoon vanilla extract
- 2 cups all-purpose flour
- 1 teaspoon baking soda
- 1 teaspoon baking powder
- 1 teaspoon salt
- 2 teaspoons cinnamon
- 1 cup canned pumpkin
- White cookie icing

Instructions

1. Preheat the oven to 350°F. Grease 2 standard cookie sheets.

2. In a large bowl, mix the sugar, egg, shortening, and vanilla extract.

3. In a medium bowl, sift together the flour, baking soda, baking powder, salt, and cinnamon. Stir into the creamed mixture and then stir in the pumpkin filling.

4. Drop the dough by rounded tablespoonfuls onto the cookie sheets.

5. Bake for 12 minutes and then let the cookies cool on cooling racks. Once cool, write each guest's first initial on a cookie with icing.

a cheese tray your way

First things first: Don't worry about the "proper way" to create a cheese tray. No matter how many do's and don'ts you've read, what really counts is that you serve the cheeses you like and that your guests will enjoy them. Here are a few tips to keep in mind as you build your next cheese platter.

know your tastes

Cheese flavors can range from sharp to mild. Sharp cheese is more bitter and pungent in taste while mild cheese is more subtle and creamy. Cheese can also have buttery, earthy, nutty, peppery, tangy, and smoky flavors. Think about which of these flavors appeal to you so that you know what to look for in a cheese.

know your audience

Now that you know the flavors you are looking for, consider your guests. You don't need to know their favorite cheeses, but you might know a little about their eating habits. Are they picky eaters? If you happen to prefer very aged or strong-smelling cheeses, you may consider offering some milder options for your friends and family who aren't quite so adventurous. Your guests will surely notice your attention to detail if you choose something for everyone.

how to buy cheese

When you are ready to purchase your cheeses, all you need to know is which types of cheese have the flavors you're looking for. Also try to vary the firmness of your cheeses to give your platter textural variety. For example, try a soft, a semi-soft, and a firm cheese for a three-cheese plate.

> The next time you go to a wine tasting or other event that features a cheese platter, don't hesitate to ask your host for information about the selections you liked best. Ask for the name of the cheese and where it was purchased.

cheese flavor and firmness guide

	Soft	Semi-Soft	Semi-Firm	Firm	Hard
Sharp	Camembert	Chantelle, Aged Muenster	Aged Serpa	Cheddar	Parmesan, Romano
Tangy	Chèvre (goat cheese)	Roquefort	Leicester	Cheshire	Kefalotyri
Nutty	Caboc	Gouda, Gorgonzola	Asiago, Swiss	Gruyère	Goya
Creamy	Neufchâtel, Brie	Havarti, Port Salut	Samso	Fontinella	Manchego
Mild	Mascarpone	Beaumont, Mozzarella	Magerkäse	Jarlsberg	Aged Farmer's Gouda

Browsing the cheese section at your local store can be overwhelming. There are many options, and they all look similar. Instead of spending $5, $10, or even $20 to find out if you like a cheese, use our cheese guide that will help you decide before you buy. Once you have some ideas, write a quick list before you shop. Then ask someone at your market to assist you in locating the cheeses. That person may be able to recommend some other types you'd like, too.

appetizing presentations

A beautiful presentation will help spark guests' interest in your platter. Try these ideas to make it as attractive as it is delicious.

- **Tier your tray.** Show off your selection as beautifully as those in a specialty shop window. It is simple to pull off: Just be creative and find ways to layer platters or boards you already have in your kitchen. If you have two wooden cutting boards, stack the smaller one on top of the larger one so that you have two different planes. For a third level, add a small plate on top.

- **Use lovely labels.** Labels help your guests know what to expect and may help some reluctant guests to try a bite of something they normally wouldn't. If your cheese set didn't come with a way to label, it is easy enough to do on your own. All you need are toothpicks, paper, a glue stick, a marker, and scissors. Cut out small flags to fold and glue around a toothpick for each type of cheese. Write the name of each cheese and a short description if you have the space. Then insert the toothpick into the cheese.

- **Utilize utensils.** Many households have a set of cheese knives. Not many know what to do with it! The reason there are so many differently shaped knives is that there are so many different textures of cheese, from soft to hard and smooth to crumbly. Use this guide (opposite) to know which cheese knife to pair with each cheese on your tray.

- **Think seasonally.** In the summer, harder cheeses are a better choice because they won't melt or sweat as much as softer varieties. Save softer, creamier cheeses for winter months.

guide to cheese knives

	The 2-tine knife is for soft and medium-hard cheeses. Cut the cheese by turning the knife on its side. Then use the pronged end for serving.
	Tear-shaped, pointed cheese knives are great for hard cheeses like Parmesan. Once split, hard cheese can crumble into chunks. Insert the tip and use only downward pressure to avoid crumbling.
	Narrow, rectangular cheese knives work best for semi-soft cheeses, like Port Salut.
	Wide, rectangular cheese knives are for soft, crumbly cheeses like goat cheese. Use it to scoop up some of the crumbles.

marvelous mango chutney

Take your entertaining to the next level by serving up this unique and fruity mango chutney as a delightful dinner party dish or create a delicious gift. Make the chutney using our simple recipe, and prepare it for serving or gift giving using a variety of fun packaging and presentation ideas. This ultimate comfort food condiment will definitely give you plenty of reasons to celebrate!

simple mango chutney

Fruity bites of mango and golden raisins are energized with ginger, vinegar, cinnamon, and sugar, and then caramelized into a golden sweet-and-sour treat that glistens like polished glass. This simple recipe will amaze your friends and family, and eliminate the mystery of the costly gourmet chutneys you've seen at the store.

MAKES ABOUT 4 CUPS

Serve the chutney as an appetizer on crackers with whipped cream cheese or on lightly battered chicken fingers. For dinner it is an amazing accompaniment for ham or turkey.

Ingredients

1 bag (12 to 16 ounces) frozen mango chunks, thawed
1½ cups white vinegar
1½ cups granulated sugar
1 box (12 to 16 ounces) golden raisins
1 teaspoon ginger
1 teaspoon nutmeg
1 teaspoon cinnamon
1 teaspoon salt

Instructions

1. Combine the ingredients in a large bowl and pour into a heavy-bottomed saucepan.

2. Bring the mixture to a boil and then lower the heat to medium.

3. Cook for 20–25 minutes, until thickened, stirring regularly to avoid scorching.

4. Chill before serving.

ham and chutney pastry

Use Simple Mango Chutney as part of this flaky baked delight. It makes an ideal entrée or appetizer for dinner parties and provides a special option for perking up everyday meals with the family. This recipe makes two pastries.

SERVES 4 AS AN ENTRÉE, 8–10 AS AN APPETIZER

Ingredients

- 1 box of 2 pie crusts (available in the dairy section of your local grocery store)
- Large baking sheet
- Parchment paper
- 4 ounces cream cheese, softened
- ¼ cup sour cream
- 2 scallions, chopped
- ¼ cup chopped onion
- 9 ounces shaved honey ham, divided
- 1 cup Simple Mango Chutney (see previous recipe), divided
- 1 tablespoon melted butter

Instructions

1. Preheat the oven to 450°F.

2. Open and unroll both pie crusts and place on a large baking sheet covered with parchment paper.

3. In a mixing bowl, combine the cream cheese, sour cream, scallions, and onion. Mix thoroughly.

4. Build the pastries burrito-style. Divide the chutney in half (½ cup each) and place each half on a pie crust lengthwise. Divide the cream cheese mixture in half and place each half on top of the chutney. Divide the ham in half and place each half on top of the cream cheese mixture.

5. Fold the pie crusts as you would a tortilla for a burrito, folding the ends in first and then the sides.

6. Flip the pastries over so that the folded sides are on the parchment.

7. Cut 3 1-inch slits in the pastries to allow them to breathe. Brush both pastries with melted butter and place in the oven until the pastry is golden brown, about 15 to 30 minutes.

8. Allow to sit for 15 minutes before cutting into sections to serve.

Serving Tips:
To serve as an entrée, cut the pastry into large rectangular sections and place a dollop of mango chutney on each plate for dipping. For a fun appetizer, cut into bite-sized squares and arrange on a serving platter. Place a small bowl of mango chutney in the center for dipping. This is great for parties and potlucks!

work space

Record your own mango chutney food pairing and gift presentation ideas here.

simple mango chutney gift ideas

Try these helpful suggestions for packaging your tasty homemade chutney as a thoughtful gift. Be sure to refrigerate before giving as a gift.

packaging ideas

1. Find fun glass containers at your local craft store or use vintage glass jars for an heirloom appeal. Wash thoroughly, spoon in the mango chutney, and attach your own unique label to the jar or tie it to the lid with a festive ribbon. Remember to include serving and storing information on the label.

2. Present your mango chutney jars inside a useful breadbasket lined with a pretty linen napkin or towel. Include a recipe card for the chutney, cream cheese, a wooden spreader, and gourmet crackers for easy snacking.

3. Put together a set of nice nested storage bowls with a jar of mango chutney inside the center bowl. Attach the chutney recipe and tie a thick velvet ribbon around the group. Your host can use the handy bowls for party leftovers for years to come.

4. Bring the chutney to a party on a serving tray or platter with a silver spreader as a gift for your host. Serve with crackers and a variety of toasted bread slices.

decorative accents

1. Measure your jar lids and cut pieces of fabric to create lovely lid covers. Tie over the lids with ribbon, raffia, or twine, and attach a sprig of dried flowers or berries.

2. Wrap the whole jar with patterned fabric, colorful tulle, tissue paper, or cellophane. Fan out over the lid and tie with ribbon. Punch a hole in a recipe card, thread a piece of ribbon through the hole, and tie.

heartfelt welcome home

There are as many good reasons to say "welcome home" as there are thoughtful ways to say it. Whether coming home from a long trip, commemorating a big accomplishment, or simply ending an ordinary day, there are lots of special ways to celebrate home, sweet home.

everyday homecoming

Sometimes a simple and unexpected greeting on a normal day can mean so much. Small gestures and easy touches prove that it is truly the thought that counts.

- There is nothing sweeter than coming home to a space smelling of fresh-baked goodies. Bake a batch of sweets, like any of our easy-to-make confections on pages 197–201, or save time by picking up their favorite treat from your local bakery.

- Music can move people like nothing else, so consider setting the mood by putting on one of their favorite songs, too. The best part? Watching their faces light up as they walk through the door.

> Your guest of honor has probably been missing his or her favorite home-cooked dishes. Make a few as a warm, delicious "welcome home" gesture.

after a big day

Do something nice for those big days, such as when a loved one gets a promotion or completes a big project. A nice welcome home reception can extend that feeling of accomplishment for days to come. There is nothing more welcoming than a fresh space. Use Febreze products to eliminate odors and leave a fresh, clean scent they'll love coming home to.

- The simplest way to commemorate a special day is with a special dinner. Make his or her favorite meal and elegantly set the table with some fresh flowers. Buy a congratulatory card or make one yourself, and put it on the table.

- When they walk through the door, make sure that the first thing they see are some words of praise. Write "Congratulations!" or "Good Job!" with a colored marker on a piece of card stock and then put it in a small picture frame. Glue or staple a pretty piece of ribbon to the two top corners on the back of the frame and then hang it over the doorknob they'll use to enter the house.

welcome home party

Make the arrival of someone who has been away from home for a long time a momentous occasion.

- Invite friends over to welcome the guest of honor in style with a full-on party. Start the soiree with a toast and then let the guest of honor talk about his or her trip so that everyone has a chance to hear the details firsthand.

- Help your loved one who has been gone a long time catch up by creating a photo album with pictures of what has been going on in the lives of friends and family members since they left. You can even include news clippings that would be of interest. After the party's over, the guest of honor can take it home to truly catch up.

> Leave a few blank pages in the back of the book so that the recipient can add photos and notes from the party as a reminder of just how good it feels to be home.

sunday morning social

The word is a mishmash, but *brunch* says exactly what it is: a combination of breakfast and lunch. It is often served on Sunday mornings when the opportunity to sleep in is best. You want your guests to keep this easy and relaxed feeling, so menus and décor should stay simple and have the go-with-the-flow attitude of a typical Sunday morning.

bouquets for brunch

There aren't many things more beautiful than a bunch of flowers sitting in the Sunday morning sun. This quick approach to décor lets the flowers do all the work while keeping things uncomplicated.

First, decide what flowers you would like as the official flower of the brunch. Blooms such as roses, orchids, and daisies are in season year-round, but you also may want to customize and use flowers that are in season, a favorite among your group, or maybe even your own favorite bud.

Then simply gather small bunches of the flower and place any number of small bouquets in bud vases or a single stem (if you're using sunflowers, for example) around your home on end tables and as centerpieces for the food display. Decorating with one type of flower or plant will help give your gathering a nice holistic feel. Tie smart, stylish ribbons around the vases for added flair.

good-morning menu

Invigorate and nourish your guests with the brunch basics: coffee, juice, muffins, and an assortment of fresh fruit. For display, find a few sturdy boxes or containers of varying heights and place them on your table (within reach of your guests, of course). Drape them with tablecloths or colorful, cool fabrics and place plates of food on top.

simple sausage scramble

Try this simple sausage scramble as a main dish.

SERVES 4–6

Ingredients

6 ounces turkey or pork sausage (casings removed)
6 eggs
¼ cup milk
Pepper to taste
1 can (14½ ounces) sliced new potatoes, drained
2 tablespoons sliced green onion
Shredded cheddar cheese (optional)

Instructions

1. Cook the sausage in a large nonstick skillet until it crumbles and is no longer pink. Drain.

2. Add the potatoes and onion to the skillet with the sausage.

3. In a medium bowl, beat together the eggs, milk, and pepper.

4. Cook over medium heat, stirring until the potatoes are cooked through and the eggs are set.

5. Serve on a plate, sprinkled with shredded cheddar cheese if desired.

breakfast bundt

Cook this versatile delight for breakfast or brunch and eat for days! It can also be paired with soup for lunch or dinner.

SERVES 8

Ingredients

2 tubes (7.5 ounces each) refrigerated buttermilk biscuits
½ pound turkey sausage, cooked and crumbled
½ pound turkey bacon, cooked and crumbled
1½ cups eggs (about 8–10), scrambled
1 cup grated reduced-fat cheddar cheese

Instructions

1. Preheat the oven to 375°F.

2. Coat a bundt pan with cooking spray and set aside.

3. Start your first layer by placing one tube of biscuits in the pan. Next, sprinkle the cooked sausage and bacon over the biscuits.

4. Pour the eggs over the meat and then sprinkle the cheese on the eggs.

5. Add the second layer of biscuits on the cheese.

6. Bake for 40 minutes. Cool and invert onto a plate to serve.

Any kind of breakfast meat can be used, such as chorizo, Italian sausage, spicy pork sausage, and Canadian bacon. Feel free to vary the type of cheese as well or substitute low-fat biscuits.

It's the breakfast that keeps on giving. Cut it into portions and freeze for later use, or use a panini press to create the perfect complement to your favorite soup at lunch or dinner.

blueberry monkey bread

Another option is to start off Sunday sweetly with this delicious monkey bread. It is a funny name, but this treat is easy to make and fun to have your guests pull off bite-sized bits of gooey sweetness.

SERVES 12

Ingredients

- 1 cup granulated sugar
- 1 tablespoon ground cinnamon
- 4 cans (10 ounces each) refrigerated buttermilk biscuit dough
- 1 cup frozen or fresh blueberries
- ¾ cup margarine or butter

Instructions

1. Preheat the oven to 350°F. Thoroughly grease a bundt pan or round cake pan. A 9" × 5½" bread pan will also do.

2. Combine the sugar and cinnamon in a bowl. Cut the biscuits into bite-sized pieces and then cover each piece with the sugar mixture.

3. Arrange a layer of biscuit pieces in the bottom of the pan. Sprinkle about one-fourth of the blueberries on top of it.

4. Repeat, adding layers of biscuit pieces and blueberries, until you reach the top of the pan.

5. Combine the rest of the sugar mixture in a saucepan with the margarine. Heat until the sugar has dissolved and the margarine has melted. Pour over the biscuits in the pan.

6. Bake for 1 hour and 15 minutes or until done. Lift and turn out onto a cake plate. Top with icing if desired.

> To add your own twist, substitute chocolate chips or strawberries for the blueberries.

burrito bar

Another great idea is to let your guests start the morning with their own recipe. Offer the option of a breakfast burrito bar containing a plate of warm corn or flour tortillas along with small dishes of all the burrito fixings: scrambled eggs, browned sausage, bacon, shredded cheese, salsa, onions, sour cream, green onions, and diced ham, to name a few.

light and fun tea party

Share tea, treats, and fun with friends and family with the following suggestions for planning a special tea party. Learn about tea party traditions, types of teas, and serving tips. Also try our deliciously light recipes. You'll be well prepared to celebrate in style.

high tea or afternoon tea?

While "high tea" may sound more regal and fancy, you may be surprised to learn it is not actually the proper name for what we picture when we think of the typical tea party. In other cultures high tea is made up of such heavy foods as meats, eggs, and cheese served at "high" tables and in place of early dinner.

Afternoon tea or "low tea" (named for being served at a smaller lounge or café-style tables) is lighter and more casual. It may be served outdoors or in a lounging area with delicate pastries, small sandwiches, and decorative tea sets.

> If the weather is gloomy, you can add a little extra whimsy to your get-together by encouraging your family and friends to wear festive floral sun hats, an old afternoon tea tradition.

your cup of tea

Amazingly, all tea leaves come from the same basic plant, *Camellia sinensis*, a type of evergreen shrub. Different tea flavors are based on how long they've been fermented and a blending of additives such as essential oils or herbs and spices.

There are three main types of teas: black (fully fermented), green (unfermented), oolong (partially fermented), and a few slight variations on those types. English Breakfast, Earl Grey, and Chai are blended teas that are often served at afternoon tea parties. Feel free to serve your personal favorites or ask your guests to bring a few teas they'd like to try or share with everyone.

brewing the perfect pot

Like the perfect pot of coffee, brewing the perfect pot of tea takes practice, but here are a few helpful tips to keep in mind:

1. Start by boiling cold, fresh water in a teakettle on your stovetop.

2. Measure out the tea: 1 tea bag or 1 teaspoon of tea leaves per 1 cup of water.

3. Add the bags or leaves (using an infuser) to the pot.

4. Follow the directions on the box or canister of tea for steeping, which can be anywhere from 1 to 5 minutes.

5. Remove the bags or leaves from the pot and serve the tea in teacups with saucers.

If you would rather let guests try teas individually, provide a teapot with hot water and let them choose their own tea bag or leaves.

> Loose tea is available at some grocery stores, coffee shops, and specialty retailers. You can also use the contents of your own favorite tea bags. Each tea bag contains about 1½ teaspoons of tea.

homemade natural teas

By getting creative with your tea leaf combinations, you can concoct new tea varieties that your guests will love. Try adding fragrant, unexpected ingredients such as fruit zest and dried flowers for deep, layered flavors. Steep the tea mixture in the teapot or in individual cups using a tea infuser, or you can pour the teas into decorative jars that your guests can tote home.

BLACK CURRANT JASMINE TEA

4 ounces black currant tea leaves
4 ounces jasmine pearl green tea leaves
2 ounces dried orange peel

LEMON MYRTLE CHAMOMILE TEA

4 ounces lemon myrtle tea leaves
4 ounces dried chamomile flowers
2 ounces dried orange peel

tea treats

At afternoon teas there are typically three main offerings: scones, English muffins, or crumpets served with jam; small savory sandwiches; and assorted pastries.

For your tea party you can serve foods according to tradition or come up with your own ideas. We have a few recipe ideas with unique twists on tradition to help make your party memorable.

chai tea squares

This decadent and delicately spiced cupcake recipe makes a perfect tea party pastry and will impress your guests with a fun presentation idea.

MAKES 16 2-INCH SQUARES

Ingredients

⅓ cup uncooked quick oatmeal (not instant)
1½ cups sifted all-purpose flour
1 teaspoon baking soda
½ teaspoon salt
1 teaspoon ground cinnamon
¾ cup light brown sugar
½ cup liquid chai concentrate (available in the tea section of your local grocery store)
½ cup milk
⅓ cup applesauce
1 tablespoon vinegar
1 teaspoon vanilla extract
½ cup flaked coconut

Instructions

1. Preheat the oven to 350°F. Grease an 8-inch square baking pan.

2. Combine the dry ingredients (oatmeal through brown sugar) in a medium-sized mixing bowl.

3. Add the chai, milk, applesauce, vinegar, vanilla extract, and coconut. Mix well and then pour the batter into the prepared pan.

4. Bake for about 25 minutes, or until a toothpick inserted in the center of the cake comes out clean.

5. This is best served warm. Cut into squares and top with Chai Mousse (see recipe below).

Serve your chai tea squares in teacups! Cut the cake with a biscuit cutter to create individual rounds. Place each round of cake in a ceramic or glass teacup and top with a heaping dollop of Chai Mousse.

chai mousse

MAKES 8 SERVINGS

Ingredients

½ cup liquid chai concentrate
1 ounce (small box) sugar-free or fat-free instant pudding, vanilla- or cheesecake-flavored
8 ounces fat-free whipped topping, well thawed

Instructions

1. Pour the chai concentrate into a 4-cup or larger measuring cup.

2. Add the pudding mix and stir with a spoon until thick and lump-free, about 1 minute.

3. Fold in the whipped topping until evenly combined.

4. Place in the refrigerator and allow to firm. Use as a topping.

cucumber pizza

You may be familiar with the bite-sized cucumber sandwiches traditionally served at fancy tea parties, so why not try something special with cucumber pizzas? These savory snacks are refreshingly simple to make.

SERVES 3–4 AS AN ENTRÉE; 6–8 AS AN APPETIZER

Ingredients

1 package of 3 mini ready-to-bake pizza crusts (available in either the dairy or bakery aisle of grocery stores)
Olive oil (enough to brush on the surface of the pizza crusts)
Whipped cream cheese, as much as desired
Mozzarella cheese, as much as desired
1 medium cucumber, peeled, diced, and chilled
Tzatziki Sauce (see recipe on page 102), chilled

Instructions

1. Preheat the oven according to the package directions on the pizza crusts.

2. Place the crusts on a parchment-lined baking sheet and brush lightly with olive oil.

3. Spread the cream cheese on the crust and top with a layer of mozzarella.

4. Place in the oven and bake until lightly browned.

5. Remove from the oven and top with the chilled cucumber and Tzatziki Sauce. Serve immediately.

tzatziki sauce

This delicious traditional Greek sauce is a versatile topping that goes great on all kinds of foods, especially cucumber pizza!

SERVES 3–4 AS AN ENTRÉE; 6–8 AS AN APPETIZER

Ingredients

12 ounces fat-free sour cream
2 cucumbers, peeled, seeded, and diced
2 tablespoons olive oil
½ lemon, juiced
Salt and pepper to taste
1 tablespoon chopped fresh dill or mint
3 cloves garlic, peeled

Instructions

1. Place all the ingredients in a food processor or blender and puree until smooth.

2. Allow to chill in the refrigerator prior to serving as a topping.

make it a bake day

Homemade cookies and bread are some of our favorite foods, but they're often the first things we skip when cooking on crunched time. So make a day of it! Have fun with your family or friends the old-fashioned way by baking the day away together. After all, lots of hands make for light work and lots of wonderful baked goods.

what's cooking?

Since you are about to make some delicious feel-good foods, invite three to five of the people in your life that make you feel good, too. Working together in the kitchen is the perfect time to laugh and share stories, regardless of age. Invite aunts, friends, nieces, and maybe even an elderly neighbor.

call for recipes

Invite guests to bring several copies of a special recipe they love and wish they had more time to bake. Some ideas are sugar cookies, cakes, muffins, biscuits, and loaves of specialty breads. Ask them if it requires special ingredients. If so, make a note of it on your next grocery list. Depending on the number of guests you invite, you may not be able to make everyone's recipes, but you can surely trade them all!

bake day prep

Before guests arrive, make sure you have plenty of such baking basics as flour, sugar, butter, eggs, and so forth. Pick up any special ingredients or arrange for your guests to bring an item or two. Since you will probably nibble on some of your baked creations, think about what you may like to offer as a complement. For breads you may like to set out some jams or honey. In the summer you could even make a bruschetta topping.

Consider setting out a few light snacks, such as hummus and pita slices, and beverages like iced tea. It is also nice to have something for your guests to fill up with baked goods on their way home. Freezer bags are inexpensive, and it is easy to store leftovers in the freezer for later.

homemade bread

If you are looking for a great recipe to start with, here's a no-fail bread recipe and three unique twists on it. If there are enough people that you decide to make several batches at once, you can even make one of each flavor.

MAKES 2 LOAVES

Ingredients

1 tablespoon granulated sugar
1 cup warm water
1 package (.25 ounce) active dry yeast
2 tablespoons butter, softened
Optional spices (see page 105)
3 cups bread flour
1 teaspoon salt
Nonstick olive oil spray

Instructions

1. In a medium bowl, dissolve the sugar in the warm water and mix in the yeast. When the yeast is foamy, mix in the butter and optional spices to flavor.

2. In a large bowl, mix the bread flour and salt. Gradually add the wet mixture and knead for 10 to 12 minutes. Be sure to keep the dough moist.

3. Spray the inside of a clean, large bowl generously with olive oil. Place the kneaded dough in the bowl, cover with a towel, and allow to rise for 1 hour in a warm place.

4. After 1 hour, punch down the dough, divide it in half, and shape the dough into 2 round loaves. Lightly spray the inside of 2 loaf pans with olive oil and place the loaves inside the pans. Cover again and allow the loaves to rise for 45 minutes to 1 hour.

5. Preheat the oven to 375°F. Make sure it is completely preheated before placing the loaves inside.

6. Bake for 15 to 20 minutes or until golden brown.

7. Take 1 loaf out of the oven and carefully remove it from the pan. Tap lightly on the bottom to check for a hollow sound. If there is no hollow sound, continue to bake, checking frequently.

8. Once done, allow the bread to cool in the pans for 30 minutes and then cool on a wire rack for 30 minutes before slicing.

three ways to spice up your bread

garden spice bread

Add these spices:
2 tablespoons finely diced fresh rosemary
2 tablespoons finely diced fresh sage

breakfast bread

Add these spices:
2 tablespoons ground cinnamon
2 tablespoons ground cloves

italian herb bread

Add these spices:
2 tablespoons basil
2 tablespoons oregano

Make a basket for a friend who couldn't be there or an elderly relative who no longer bakes for herself or himself.

grilled summer shortcake

Grill your fruit for intensified flavor that enhances the traditional short-cake. By taking dessert to the grill, you'll create a deliciously different treat your friends and family won't be able to resist.

SERVES 4

> Prep time: 30 minutes
> Bake time: 10 minutes

Ingredients

SHORTCAKES

> ¾ cup flour
> 2 tablespoons sugar
> 1½ teaspoons baking powder
> ⅛ teaspoon salt
> ½ cup heavy cream, plus more for brushing
> ½ teaspoon vanilla extract
> 1 tablespoon brown sugar

GRILLED FRUIT

> Canola oil
> 2 peaches, cut in half, pits removed
> 2 plums, cut in half, pits removed
> 12 large strawberries, hulled (or other berries of your choice)
> ¼ cup brown sugar

TOPPING

> Sweetened whipped cream (optional)

Instructions

1. Preheat oven to 375°F. In a medium mixing bowl, combine flour, sugar, baking powder and salt. Mix well.

2. In an electric mixer, whip cream with vanilla until soft peaks form. Add flour mixture to cream and beat on low until well blended.

3. Turn dough onto a lightly floured surface and knead gently. Pat dough into a 6-inch circle.

4. Lightly brush dough with cream, then sprinkle with brown sugar. Cut into 4 wedges.

5. Transfer to a baking sheet and bake until golden brown for about 10 minutes. Cool before removing from sheet.

A variety of berries like raspberries, blueberries, and blackberries are plentiful during summer months and can be substituted for personalized flavor. Skewers are recommended for smaller berries that could fall through the grill.

6. Heat grill to medium high. Lightly brush fruit with oil. Grill peaches and plums for about 8 minutes, turning frequently until juicy and grill marked. Add strawberries to the grill during last minute of cooking.

7. When cool enough to handle, cut peaches and plums into chunks. Toss with brown sugar and gently stir in strawberries. Let stand 5 minutes.

8. Split shortcakes in half, and place the bottom halves on dessert plates. Top with fruit, sweetened whipped cream, and the top half of the shortcake. Serve.

baked goods to go

At the end of the day, divide up all your delicious treats. Everyone can take some items to eat fresh and some to freeze for the coming months. Fill freezer bags and mark each one with the date. And don't forget to swap your recipes!

spring fiesta

In the springtime coax your family and friends from their winter cocoons with a vibrant, high-energy spring fiesta. It is a wonderful way to celebrate the beginning of a bright and sunny season. Try these fun food, drink, and decoration ideas to create a bold, beautiful, and interactive spring party.

first "to-do"

Make a guest list and send out a detailed e-invite, complete with date, time, and a description of your fiesta theme. Let everyone know that this simple and creative gathering will be complete with all your unique personal touches. Invite them to make their favorite salsa recipe (and chips) to bring along.

surprise salsa contest

Prepare for the salsa contest by arranging a secret ballot "salsa sampler," which will take place during the party. Guests will sample the salsas and vote for their favorite. You can even offer the winner a prize, such as a lovely spring bouquet, a chip and salsa serving dish, or a gift certificate to a favorite Mexican or Spanish restaurant.

decorations

There is only one way to go with fiesta décor: simple, sparkly, and hot. Think lots of small twinkling lights and bright, gorgeous colors. Pretty cacti and piñata party lights or multicolored holiday lights can really heat up a room. For added ambiance pick up some beautiful spring flowers and create a few free-spirited centerpieces or mini bouquets to place around the room on end tables, bookshelves, and counters.

flowers for her hair

April showers bring May flowers. After the ambiance is set, welcome guests to the party with a simple, pretty, and vibrant flower. Arrange a bundle of beautiful spring flowers near the entrance and have guests choose a single bloom as they arrive. Encourage women to put the flower in their hair, while men can wear it as a small boutonniere.

spicy snacks

The décor is set, the guests have arrived, and everyone is ready to celebrate. Spirited fare will help break the ice and get the party warmed up. Concoct a few quick batches of your own homemade salsa and display them as a salsa bar. Here is a selection of sweet, spicy, and vegetable salsas to get you started.

simple southwest fruit salsa

Try this fruit salsa with tortilla chips for a sweet treat. It is also a great accompaniment to grilled chicken, fish, steaks, pork, or lamb chops.

MAKES ABOUT 2½ CUPS

Ingredients
1 can (15 ounces) mixed fruit, drained
½ cup coarsely chopped red onion
2 tablespoons chopped fresh cilantro
1½ tablespoons fresh lime juice
1 teaspoon seeded and chopped jalapeño pepper (fresh or canned)

Instructions
Combine all ingredients in a bowl. Let stand at room temperature at least 15 minutes or refrigerate up to 6 hours before serving.

> Nearly any canned fruit, even those packed in syrup, can be used in this salsa recipe. If you use peaches, pears, apricots, or pineapple, make sure the fruit is diced for the salsa.

quick corn-pineapple salsa

For a heartier option, throw together this quick salsa idea. It also goes great with broiled chicken breast and broiled salmon fillet as a main course.

MAKES ABOUT 3½ CUPS

Ingredients

1 can (15¼ ounces) whole kernel golden sweet corn, drained
1 can (8 ounces) crushed pineapple in its own juice, drained
½ cup chopped green and/or red sweet pepper
¼ cup chopped fresh cilantro
1 seeded and finely chopped jalapeño pepper (optional)

Instructions

Stir all the ingredients together in a medium bowl. Garnish with additional cilantro and jalapeño peppers if desired.

Make cleaning your salsa bowls and drink glasses easy with Cascade. Your dishes will come out clean and beautiful every time!

---

salsa vera cruz

Give your taste buds a little kick. This quick salsa will spice up mixed green salads and tortilla or pita chips. Top with grilled shrimp and rice, too, for a delicious dinner.

MAKES ABOUT 4½ CUPS

Ingredients

1 can (14½ ounces) diced tomatoes with mild green chilies
1 orange, peeled and chopped
¼ cup sliced green onions
¼ cup chopped cilantro or parsley
1 cup salsa
1 tablespoon olive oil
1 to 2 tablespoons minced jalapeño pepper
Salt and pepper (optional)

Instructions

Combine the undrained tomatoes, orange, onions, cilantro, salsa, oil, and jalapeño pepper in a medium bowl. Season to taste with salt and pepper, if desired.

sea foam

After eating all that hot salsa, your guests will need drinks to cool off. Serve this tasty and yet low-calorie and low-sugar refreshment that is sure to help keep the party going. See also Sweet and Simple No-Bake Desserts on page 193.

SERVES 3

Ingredients

½ honeydew melon, seeded and scooped
1 cucumber, peeled and sliced
¼ cup lime juice
¼ cup fresh mint leaves
¼ cup granulated sugar
Chilled grapefruit citrus soda

Instructions

1. Place the melon, cucumber, lime juice, mint leaves, and sugar in a blender and puree until smooth.

2. Force through a strainer, reserving the juice and disposing of the pulp.

3. Chill for 4 hours or overnight.

4. Fill each glass with one-third of the melon mixture and top with the grapefruit citrus soda.

host a progressive tapas party

Host the type of tapas party that your friends can really get into. A progressive dinner, in which each course takes place at a different location, is a great way to keep the night interesting without all the stress of being a lone hostess. And the best part? No one is left to make a main dish!

the basics

Tapas are a Spanish tradition that is becoming popular around the world. Tapas are small, bite-sized snacks that are meant to be shared and savored. Basically, they are similar to heavy appetizers, so all your guests have to do is make a hearty appetizer or two. Mini shish kebabs, warm dips, cheese platters, and even fondue are perfect for this tasty evening event.

step one: guest list

The first thing you'll want to do is decide whom you'd like to invite. Consider inviting five to seven couples, expecting that three to five couples will be able to attend. It is easiest when all your guests live close together so that they all can hop from one destination to another. Walking distance is best, but a short drive between each destination shouldn't be too much trouble. It is a great way to bring your neighbors together if friends don't live near enough.

   Each couple can make a dish or two. With fewer couples, such as three or four, each pair should cook two or even three dishes to make sure everyone gets enough to eat. Decide where each home falls in your progressive "route" and then let guests know so they can plan their dishes accordingly. Set yourself for the end of the route so that you can host the "after party."

work space

Here's the perfect spot to plan your progressive party.

Couple	Address	Tapas

step two: route

Send invitations at least three to four weeks ahead or call everyone for a more casual approach. Just make sure each person RSVPs so that you know your total number of participants. This way everyone has a better idea of how much food to prepare.

step three: final dish, dessert, and drinks

Now it is time to start planning your dishes. As the final destination, you should offer a final appetizer and a few different desserts and after-dinner beverages. For inspiration see the Crispy Cinnamon Sugar Palmiers, Apricot Pine Nut Shortbread Diamonds, Ganache-Glazed Brownie Bars, and Chocolate Ganache in La Dolce Vita on page 197.

stuffed and roasted baby bellas

Consider this easy recipe for your final appetizer. Stuffed and Roasted baby bella mushrooms are a delicious way to finish off the savory selections before moving on to dessert.

SERVES 4–6

Ingredients

1 package (8 ounces) whole baby bella mushrooms
Soy sauce
Freshly ground pepper
1 package (4 ounces) blue cheese crumbles

Instructions

1. Preheat the oven to 400°F.

2. Wash and de-stem the mushrooms. Place them, cap down, on a baking sheet.

3. Drizzle the mushrooms with soy sauce and dust with black pepper.

4. Bake for 30 minutes.

5. Remove from the oven and fill the mushrooms with blue cheese crumbles. Return them to the oven to bake for an additional 10 minutes or until the cheese has fully melted.

Chances are your stuffed mushrooms will disappear quickly, but to keep extras hot, try serving them on a flat electric skillet.

grilled artichokes with lemon mayo

Artichokes are a tasty, nutrient-rich vegetable with lots of potential for creative cooking. Try tossing artichokes on the grill for a scrumptious side dish or appetizer that pairs perfectly with tangy lemon mayo.

SERVES 2-4

Prep time: 10 minutes
Cook time: 10 minutes

Ingredients

LEMON MAYO

½ cup mayonnaise
Zest of 1 lemon
2 tablespoons lemon juice
1 teaspoon Dijon mustard
Dash of hot sauce

GRILLED ARTICHOKES

2 large artichokes, rinsed well, top third removed and leaf tips trimmed
½ cup olive oil
2 tablespoons balsamic vinegar
1 clove garlic, minced
Salt and pepper, to taste

Instructions

1. Combine mayonnaise, lemon zest, lemon juice, Dijon mustard, and hot sauce in a mixing bowl. Mix, then cover and store in the refrigerator to be served with grilled artichokes.

2. Place artichokes with their stem side up in a large microwave-safe bowl. Drizzle 1 tablespoon of water on artichokes, then cover tightly with plastic wrap.

3. Microwave 8–10 minutes or until just tender and an outer leaf easily pulls out.

4. Remove plastic wrap and let stand until cool enough to handle. Cut artichokes into halves or quarters and discard the inner prickly purple leaves and hairy choke.

5. In a bowl, combine the olive oil, vinegar, and garlic. Add artichokes and turn gently to coat. Let stand while heating the grill to medium high.

6. Remove artichokes from the marinade and place them on the grill. Turn for about 5 minutes until warmed through and lightly charred around the edges.

7. Place on a serving platter and season with salt and pepper to taste. Serve with Lemon Mayo on the side for dipping.

step four: final touches

About a week before the party, check with friends to make sure there are no repeat dishes. Also let them know where the party will start and when they can plan on the time line for the group to arrive at their home while house jumping. Now think about preparing your space. For party décor ideas, see Inexpensive Ideas, Beautiful Results on page 69.

Whatever the special occasion, nothing says congratulations like a bundle of goodies presented in a decorative basket. From wedding gestures to well wishes, get inspired by the big day at hand and craft a gift basket that lets a loved one know he or she is in your thoughts. Take a cue from our themed ideas and then continue to reinvent the gift basket as new milestones arise.

for a friend

Imagine your friend's delight when you surprise her with a customized gift basket for her birthday, engagement, or other special day:

- **Into the Garden:** From homeowners to city dwellers, it seems everyone wants a green thumb these days. Assemble a gardening starter kit, complete with an instructional book, gardening gloves, soil, and the seeds of her favorite flower. Arrange everything within a painted terra-cotta pot from which she can grow her new plants.

- **Circle of Friends:** Does your friend surround herself with inspiring people? Consider enlisting them to craft small one-of-a-kind gifts that can be compiled together—perhaps an artistic pair of earrings from a coworker's side business, a landscape photograph taken by a neighbor, or a scarf knitted by her younger sister. Place everything inside a simple glass container, such as a vase or fish bowl, so that no detail is missed. Top the arrangement with tissue paper or a decorative bow.

for the graduate

If you are stumped as to what to give someone who is college bound, try creating an arrangement that is equal parts fun, memories, and function:

- **Survival Kit:** Compile items that will get lots of use once the student sets foot on campus. Consider prepaid gift cards for online music stores, long-distance phone calls, the school bookstore, or a favorite take-out restaurant.

- **Perfectly Packaged:** Encase your gifts in something academically inspired such as a backpack, slouchy purse, or laptop case. Add a finishing touch with a fabric bow or overflow the open zipper side with colorful tissue paper for a pop of color.

for the bride

When it comes to nuptials, buying from the registry is the typical route. But if you're feeling like a renegade gift giver, consider a gift basket as a creative, personalized alternative. Here are some suggestions:

- **Sew Perfect:** Fill a sewing basket with straight pins, needles, thread, thimbles, measuring tape, and scissors. Add the bride's favorite yarn, fabrics, or craft supplies, too. Then customize the sewing basket on the outside with little touches that speak to the bride's unique personality.

- **A Clean Start:** While it sounds boring, giving the married couple a collection of cleaning supplies is a thoughtful detail-oriented gift; it is perfect as a second gesture to accompany your main present. After all, household chores can be a cause of newlywed stress. Give the couple a starter kit of cleaning supplies wrapped inside a convenient carry caddy. This way they can carry all their supplies with them from room to room as they complete their chores.

- **Food Finds:** Couples everywhere are cooking together, so consider giving a great food resource: a subscription to a newspaper's weekly food section. You might also add the Sunday section from another favorite newspaper, along with a subscription to the couple's favorite niche magazine. Place all the subscription cards in a beautiful flower arrangement or design your own flower bouquet from old newspapers and magazine pages for an unexpected touch. For ideas on creating your own floral designs, see Do-It-Yourself Flower Power on page 311.

> **Tweak the idea of a gift basket by creating one composed of lots of small, sweet gifts handcrafted by you. Consider making a fabric-bound journal, a beaded friendship bracelet, or a set of decoupaged place mats.**

clever kitchen

cook. eat. smile. repeat.

Home is where your heart is, and your kitchen is the heart of the home. It's the place where you cook the meals that nourish your family and feed your soul. It's the room where loved ones gather to talk about their day, steal a taste of your latest dish, and maybe even stick around to set the table.

We'll help you make this all-important space an organized haven so that you can focus on getting into the culinary spirit. Once your kitchen is clean, comfortable, and efficient, you'll be ready to whip up a quick Monday night meal or make an appetite-enticing creation for a special occasion.

Cooking doesn't have to be complicated, and you don't have to be a master chef to put love into your meals and smiles on the faces of your family and friends. With our simple tips, tricks, and recipes you'll have fun getting food on the table and feel confident about it, too.

plan a week of delicious dinners

Some people know what they're going to make for dinner five days ahead. Others wonder what's for supper up until the moment they start making it. Whichever type you are, planning your weekly menu in advance is a smart money-saving approach to the dinner table that results in fewer trips to the grocery store and tastier, healthier meals.

The secret to planning a meal menu for the week is to start small and simple. Just think about next week—seven breakfasts, lunches, and dinners, plus a few snacks thrown in. Remember, the longer you plan your weekly menus, the better you'll become.

start with the deals

A good place to begin your menu planning is with the weekly grocery circular in your local newspaper.

After you have seen what the savings are, set your menu accordingly, knowing that, for example, you can save money by cooking chicken breasts instead of pork loins. It is a tactic that can give way to big inspirations in the kitchen: When you focus on creating meals around certain ingredients, you can generate an idea for a meal you haven't tried before.

consider your schedule

Once you have taken your grocery store's deals into account, start rounding out your meal plan—but don't start with the food, start with the week. What are your plans? Are you responsible for the carpool on Tuesday evening? Is Wednesday going to be an especially busy day at work, leaving you with little energy for a big meal? Are friends coming over on Saturday?

Also take into consideration your cooking routines. Is Friday always pizza night? Do you like to spend more time preparing a bigger meal on Sunday? With these details in mind, start filling in your weekly meal-planning work space.

> **For major savings you can also visit your local grocery store's Web site, where weekly saving coupons are often featured and ready to print.**

work space

Soon, weekly menu planning will be second nature. For now, practice a weekly meal calendar here.

_____

Monday

_____

Tuesday

_____

Wednesday

_____

Thursday

_____

Friday

_____

Saturday

_____

Sunday

_____

an empty pantry

Once you have your menu planned, make a grocery list of every ingredient you'll need. Pretend that you don't have a thing in your kitchen and write down every possible component. After you have a complete grocery list, look in your pantry and refrigerator, and cross off the items that you have on hand (and are still fresh).

After taking inventory, fill out the shopping list on the right-hand side of the menu planner with the ingredients you still need to purchase. Take this list with you to do your grocery shopping.

a valuable kitchen accessory

When you arrive home, hang your menu on the fridge so you'll be reminded of the meals that are coming up. Remember, just because you've set up the week's menu doesn't mean you have to follow it to a tee. You might find a great deal as you walk through the grocery store that wasn't in the newspaper. Or maybe your schedule gets thrown off on Tuesday night and suddenly pizza night needs to happen tonight. The menu is there to help you, not limit you.

Give yourself a few weeks to get the hang of menu planning, and then you'll realize just how helpful it is. With all your ingredients on hand, you can prepare fresh, healthy dishes with ease. And best of all, you can kiss those last-minute trips to the grocery good-bye.

farmers' market finds

Buying local produce supports local farms and helps us stay connected to fresh seasonal flavors. Plus, local produce has usually traveled less than a day from farm to store or market; meaning that costs saved in transportation get passed on to you. Fruits and vegetables add vibrant colors and great nutrition to meals, and we choose to focus on two summertime staples: tomatoes and berries. To find out when your favorite fruits and veggies are in season, just do a quick online search or ask a local grower.

picking the best tomatoes

Tomatoes peak during summer months. Locally grown tomatoes usually have the best flavor because they ripen completely on the vine. When shopping for tomatoes at a store or farmers' market, look for selections that are smooth, well ripened (slightly soft and bright in color), and mostly free from blemishes.

heirloom tomatoes

Heirloom tomatoes are especially abundant during summer months. They come in hundreds of varieties, shapes, flavors, and colors. Each variety has its own story and history that gets handed down through generations. Small local farms and backyard gardeners are more likely to cultivate heirlooms, which is why farmers' markets are often the best places to find them.

stacked heirloom tomato sandwich

This is a farmers' market version of the classic BLT. This open-faced sandwich is perfect for the summer. If heirloom tomatoes are not available, try using fresh vine-ripened tomatoes. You may even be able to find a variety of vine-ripened colors such as yellow and green.

MAKES 4 OPEN-FACED SANDWICHES

Ingredients

2 ounces bacon (approximately 4 slices)
4 slices crusty bread (sourdough or French baguette)
Olive oil
Salt and pepper or Italian seasoning blend to taste
4 medium heirloom tomatoes in assorted colors,
    cut into ¼–⅓-inch slices
20 small, fresh basil leaves, chopped
1½ ounces blue cheese, crumbled
Balsamic or red wine vinaigrette

Instructions

1. Thoroughly cook the bacon in a heavy skillet over medium heat until crisp. Transfer to a paper towel to drain.

2. Brush each bread slice with olive oil and sprinkle with salt and pepper or an Italian seasoning blend. Bake in the oven at 400°F for 3 to 5 minutes. Remove and place on a cooling rack.

3. Crumble the bacon. Place one slice of toasted bread on each plate and divide the tomato slices among them, sprinkling some of the bacon and basil between the slices.

4. Top with the remaining bacon, basil, and blue cheese. Drizzle your favorite balsamic or red wine vinaigrette dressing over the tomatoes and serve.

> To make this recipe vegetarian, simply omit the bacon or choose a soy-based alternative such as soy bacon (available at specialty stores or in natural food sections).

> If blue cheese isn't your favorite, try crumbled Gorgonzola, feta, goat cheese, or fresh sliced mozzarella.

farm-fresh berries

The very best berries are available during the summer, including black-berries, raspberries, blueberries, and strawberries.

When you shop, look for berries that are firm, plump, and free from moisture. Avoid berries that aren't quite the color they're supposed to be—for example, strawberries with white or green spots. This means that they may not have fully ripened. Also, stay away from stained containers, which may mean the berries are bruised or rotting.

storing berries

All berries are highly perishable and should be stored in the refrigerator and used within three days to a week at most. Use these basic tips as a guideline:

- Ripe raspberries, strawberries, and blueberries should be stored in a sealed container.

- Blackberries can be stored uncovered.

- Soft or blemished berries should be removed from containers to keep other berries from spoiling.

- Storing berries between paper towels will help keep them dry.

work space

Use this space to record when your favorite fruits
and vegetables are in season.

angelic berry trifle

Use your farm-fresh berries for this flavorful layered treat that's as simple as it is impressive. Using angel food cake makes it a lighter dessert for hot summer nights.

SERVES 6

Ingredients

8 ounces blueberries
8 ounces strawberries, sliced
8 ounces red raspberries
8 ounces blackberries
½ cup water
½ cup sugar
2 teaspoons cornstarch
Lemon juice, to preserve freshness of the fruit
Store-bought angel food cake, sliced ½-inch thick

LEMON CUSTARD

1 cup cold water
1 package (8-servings) instant lemon pudding
16 ounces whipped cream topping

Instructions

1. Place half of each variety of berries in a large bowl. Sprinkle with lemon juice and set aside.

2. Combine the remaining berries, water, sugar, and cornstarch in a saucepan over medium-high heat. Bring to a simmer and cook about 3 minutes, just until the berries begin to break down and release juices. Remove the berries from the heat and let cool to thicken the mixture.

3. In a clean bowl, stir the cold water and instant lemon pudding together until smooth. Fold in the whipped cream topping.

4. To assemble the trifle, spoon a layer of the lemon custard into individual glass serving cups. Add a layer of angel food cake, breaking the slices into chunks. Then soak the cake with a layer of the berry juice mixture. Top with the reserved fresh berries and serve.

why cook it that way?

One recipe may tell you to sauté while another instructs you to poach. There are good reasons to do as the recipes say, of course, but most cooks don't know exactly what they are. Learn the differences and how each method brings out wonderful flavors in your meats. Soon you'll be empowered with simple concepts that you can apply in your everyday cooking. Test your knowledge with these savory recipes.

so they say to sauté

"Sauté" literally translates to "jump." In the kitchen it simply means to cook on a stove in a pan with a small amount of oil or butter over medium-high or high heat. The method is to keep the food moving frequently. This method is often confused with searing, which means to leave the meat still in a single spot to cook the surface.

macadamia nut–encrusted chicken

This is a simple and delicious example of sautéed chicken. For a great side to pair with this dish, try Roasted Vegetable Risotto Salad with Lemon Vinaigrette on page 188.

SERVES 4

Ingredients

4 chicken breasts
1 cup flour
4 eggs, beaten
2 cups ground macadamia nuts
3 teaspoons sea salt or kosher salt
3 teaspoons freshly ground pepper
¼ cup vegetable oil

Instructions

1. First, get ready to bread the chicken. Place the flour, eggs, and macadamia nuts in 3 separate bowls, all of which should be large enough to fit a chicken breast.

2. Place the chicken on a plate and lightly sprinkle each piece with salt and pepper.

3. Roll one piece of chicken in the flour. Then dip it into the egg and roll in the ground macadamia nuts. Make sure to coat the chicken evenly. Repeat until all the chicken pieces are breaded.

4. Place the chicken in the refrigerator for 10 minutes. This gives the egg time to bind the flour and nuts to the chicken.

5. In a large nonstick pan, bring the oil to medium heat. Before dropping in a whole piece of chicken, test a breading crumb first. Look for it to bubble and lightly cook.

6. Cook all 4 pieces of chicken in the pan at once. Cook both sides, turning frequently, for a total of 20 minutes.

hear to sear?

Searing is a method of panfrying. To sear, you cook your meat in a little butter, oil, or grease over high heat for a short time. This method caramelizes the outside of the meat, keeping it tender and locking in the juices. Searing also gives the meat a beautiful color and a nice crust. Baking after searing cooks the protein thoroughly. And for those stovetop spills, Mr. Clean is the perfect remedy.

seared pork chops

This simple recipe takes little time and few ingredients but delivers a beautiful juicy dish. If you would like to serve your pork chops on a bed of couscous, see Create Your Own Couscous on page 173.

SERVES 4

Ingredients

4 pork chops
3 teaspoons salt
3 teaspoons freshly ground black pepper
3 teaspoons Italian seasoning
¼ cup vegetable oil

Instructions

1 Preheat the oven to 375°F.

2. In a bowl, combine the salt, pepper, and Italian seasoning. Sprinkle on both sides of the pork chops.

3. In a large sauté pan, heat the oil over high heat.

4. Place the pork chops in the pan. Be careful because the hot oil may pop. As the pork chops cook, watch them change colors. Once you see a nicely defined brown spot on the first side, it's time to flip the pork chop. Use tongs so that you're less likely to splatter oil. Cook until nicely browned.

5. Place the pork chops on a sheet tray and bake for 15 minutes.

6. Remove the pork from the oven. Allow 4 to 5 minutes before serving so that the juices have time to settle back into the meat.

> Sometimes it can be hard to tell when your oil is ready for searing. When you see the oil flowing around the pan, you know that it's hot and ready to go. If it starts to smoke, that means it's slightly too hot.

the recipe reads "roast"

Roasting is a method of placing meat in the oven so that direct heat cooks the protein from all sides. This technique really brings the bold, golden flavor out in meat. It is also the easiest of the cooking methods.

pork tenderloin roast

Experience how well this method brings out the natural flavors of a pork tenderloin. All you need are basic spices to enhance the already rich taste. Wow guests at a dinner party by presenting this mouthwatering pork tenderloin as your main course.

SERVES 4

Ingredients

- 4 tablespoons olive oil
- 3 teaspoons salt
- 3 teaspoons freshly ground black pepper
- 1 teaspoon ground cayenne pepper
- 1 pork tenderloin

Instructions

1. Preheat the oven to 375°F.

2. Combine all the ingredients in a bowl except for the tenderloin.

3. Mix well and pour over the meat, making sure to coat well.

4. Place the coated tenderloin on a sheet tray and place in the oven to roast for 25 to 30 minutes.

5. Remove from the oven and allow to rest for 5 minutes before slicing.

when coached to poach

Poaching, also known as braising, means cooking meat in liquid. This is the easiest way to keep your protein tender and moist. Poaching in plain water doesn't give much flavor to the dish, so it's best to add flavorful ingredients to the water.

chicken salad with toasted pecans and red grapes

Bring a little more flavor to this classic salad by poaching the chicken with herbs and spices. You are sure to notice the difference. Serve on croissants for a light meal or with finger food for an occasion such as the Light and Fun Tea Party on page 96.

SERVES 4

Ingredients

> 6 cups water
> 1 cup lemon juice
> 1 cup dry white wine
> 1 tablespoon whole peppercorns
> 1 bay leaf
> 4 chicken breasts
> 2 cups halved red grapes
> ½ cup toasted pecans
> ¼ cup diced celery
> ¼ cup diced white onion
> 2 teaspoons ground thyme
> 2 cups mayonnaise

Instructions

1. In a large stockpot, combine the water, lemon juice, wine, peppercorns, and bay leaf. Bring to a boil.

2. Add the chicken to the pot and lower the heat to medium-high.

3. Cook the chicken for 20 minutes, until it floats to the top of the water. Remove and set aside to dry and cool.

Another technique is to poach or braise in a flavored liquid, such as broth or even fruit juice, instead of water.

4. In a large bowl, combine the grapes, pecans, onion, celery, and thyme with the mayonnaise. Set aside.

5. Shred the chicken with a fork.

6. Fold the chicken into the mayonnaise mixture. Now just let your salad cool before serving by the scoop on a bed of greens or on bread for a sandwich.

The idea of "putting food out" when guests come over makes it sound so easy—as though any food would do as long as it's out. But with these recipes for chips and dips, it is almost that easy—not to mention delicious. These recipes will make your finger foods the highlight of your next party.

All these recipes are simple to pull together, with only a few minutes of active prep time before they either go in the oven or on the table. You'll have plenty of time to get the rest of your home party-ready and have a little something for everyone to enjoy.

simple pita crisps

If you are going to have dips, you'll need something to dip in them. While fresh raw vegetables are always a great option, these simple pita crisps provide another healthy choice for your yummy dips.

MAKES ABOUT 8 DOZEN

Ingredients

12 pita bread pockets
½ cup olive oil
½ teaspoon ground black pepper
1 teaspoon garlic salt
½ teaspoon dried parsley

Instructions

1. Preheat the oven to 400°F.

2. Cut each pita bread pocket into triangles, about 8 per pita. Place the triangles on a lined cookie sheet.

3. Combine the oil, pepper, garlic salt, and parsley in a small bowl. Brush the mixture on one side of each triangle.

4. Bake in the oven about 7 minutes, or until the corners are lightly browned and crispy.

cheesy onion dip

This warm onion dip is so easy to make—just chop, mix, and bake. Try serving it in a bread bowl: Simply cut off the top of a round loaf of pumpernickel or sourdough bread and scoop out the middle to make a bowl.

MAKES ABOUT 5 CUPS

Ingredients

1½ cups chopped Vidalia onion
½ cup chopped green onion
1 clove garlic, minced
1 cup mayonnaise
1 cup shredded provolone cheese
1 cup shredded Parmesan cheese
Chunks of bread

Instructions

1. Preheat the oven to 350°F.

2. Thoroughly mix together the onions, garlic, mayonnaise, and cheese in a medium bowl. Transfer to a small casserole dish.

3. Bake for 30 minutes in the oven until the onions are tender and the top is golden.

4. Serve in the casserole dish or in a bread bowl with chunks of bread for dipping.

spinach artichoke dip

Spinach dips are among the most popular at parties, but this recipe uses artichoke hearts and Alfredo sauce to add a new taste to an old favorite.

MAKES ABOUT 4 CUPS

Ingredients

1 can (14 ounces) artichoke hearts, drained and chopped
½ package (10 ounces) frozen chopped spinach, thawed
¼ cup sour cream
¼ cup mayonnaise
½ cup Alfredo sauce
¼ cup shredded Italian cheese mix
¼ teaspoon minced garlic
Tortilla chips or pita crisps for dipping

Instructions

1. Preheat the oven to 375°F.

2. Mix together all the ingredients except the chips or crisps in a small baking dish and cover.

3. Bake until heated through and bubbly, about 25 minutes.

4. Serve in the warm dish or in a serving bowl with the tortilla chips or pita crisps on the side.

hummus made simple

This popular Middle Eastern dish goes great with raw vegetables. Be sure to make enough, because it will go quickly.

MAKES ABOUT 2½ CUPS

Ingredients

- 1 can (19 ounces) garbanzo beans (also called chickpeas), drained
- 4 tablespoons lemon juice
- 2 tablespoons tahini
- 2 cloves garlic, chopped
- 2 tablespoons olive oil

Instructions

1. Rinse the garbanzo beans and pour them into a blender or food processor. Add the lemon juice, tahini, and garlic. Blend or process until creamy and well mixed.

2. Transfer the mixture to a medium-sized serving bowl. Pour the olive oil over the top. Serve with raw vegetables.

This recipe calls for tahini, a sesame seed paste that is similar to peanut butter. You can find it in ethnic and specialty food stores as well as in the ethnic food section of most large grocery stores.

warm crab and cheese dip

In a few simple steps you can blend together a seafood-inspired dip that is accented with a touch of spice. You can pour it into a rustic bread bowl or pair it with pita crisps and vegetables.

MAKES ABOUT 3 CUPS

Ingredients

- 8 ounces lump crabmeat
- 8 ounces cream cheese, softened
- 1 cup grated sharp cheddar cheese
- ¼ teaspoon ground nutmeg
- 1 teaspoon hot sauce
- 1 round loaf bread, hollowed out

Instructions

1. Preheat the oven to 350°F. In a large mixing bowl, blend together the crabmeat, cream cheese, cheddar cheese, nutmeg, and hot sauce with a hand mixer or spoon.

2. Pour the mixture into a soufflé dish and bake in the oven for approximately 20 minutes, or until bubbling and golden brown.

3. Remove the dish from the oven and pour the dip into the bread bowl. Serve warm with bread cubes, chips, and vegetables for dipping.

Get playful with your ingredients: Consider replacing the cheddar cheese with Parmesan, Asiago, or Gruyère. You can even add black beans, corn, and chopped bell peppers right into your dip.

Warm Crab and Cheese Dip can be made up to three days in advance. Simply refrigerate in a bowl sealed with plastic wrap and then, when ready to serve, remove the plastic wrap and bake the dip.

sensational salads

Meals made at home are best when they're quick, refreshing, and simple—and so are these salads! Best of all, you can get them to the table in 20 minutes or less. Once you have mastered the basics, use our simple suggestions for taking them from sensational sides to enticing entrées for lunch or dinner.

To substitute an ingredient with what you have on hand or for a different flavor, try almonds in place of the pine nuts and basil in place of the mint.

fresh watermelon salad

Mix together a savory and sweet combination of juicy watermelon, feta cheese, and pine nuts. Finish with a balsamic dressing.

MAKES ABOUT 4½ CUPS, SERVES 4–6

Ingredients

4 cups seedless watermelon, diced in ½-inch to ¾-inch pieces
¼ cup pine nuts, toasted
2 tablespoons white balsamic vinegar, or more to taste
½ cup (4 ounces) feta cheese, crumbled
2 tablespoons chopped fresh mint
Freshly ground black pepper to taste

Instructions

1. Combine the watermelon, pine nuts, and vinegar in a large bowl and toss.

2. Top with the feta cheese, mint, and ground pepper.

3. Transfer to plates and serve immediately.

Make this salad into an entrée by adding chicken, pork, or lamb.

orzo garden salad

This consists of simple rice-shaped pasta, crisp zucchini, carrots, and celery mixed with juicy tomatoes, fragrant herbs, Parmesan cheese, and a light oil dressing. Raid your own vegetable garden for fresh additions or substitutions.

SERVES 4

Ingredients

- 1 cup dry orzo pasta
- 1 small zucchini, chopped
- 1 medium carrot, thinly sliced
- 2 medium stalks of celery, chopped
- 1 tablespoon finely chopped shallot
- ¼ cup chopped Roma tomatoes
- 1 teaspoon chopped fresh basil
- 1 teaspoon oregano
- 1 tablespoon olive oil
- 1 tablespoon red wine vinegar
- 2 tablespoons grated Parmesan cheese or more to taste

Make the Orzo Garden Salad into an entrée by adding chicken or tofu.

Instructions

1. Cook the orzo according to the package instructions.

2. While the orzo cooks, boil about 1 inch of water in a medium saucepan. Add the vegetables except the tomatoes and cover with a lid. Lower the heat and simmer about 3 minutes or until tender.

3. Drain and rinse the vegetables under cold water. Do the same with the orzo.

4. Combine the vegetables, including the tomatoes, basil, and oregano with the orzo in a large bowl. Mix well.

5. Combine the oil, vinegar, and Parmesan in a small bowl. Pour the dressing over the mixed salad.

6. Cover and refrigerate until ready to serve.

nutty edamame salad

Edamame (soybeans) are a great source of fiber and protein and the perfect addition to any salad. You can find them already shelled in the freezer section.

SERVES 4

Ingredients

1 pound shelled edamame
1 red bell pepper, chopped
2 scallions, chopped
¼ cup finely chopped red onion
2 tablespoons chopped mint
¼ cup unsalted sliced almonds (or chopped cashews), toasted
2 tablespoons sesame oil
1 tablespoon red wine vinegar
2 tablespoons soy sauce
½ teaspoon chili sauce
Freshly ground pepper to taste (optional)

Instructions

1. Place the shelled edamame in a pot of salted boiling water for 3 to 5 minutes.

2. Drain, rinse with cold water, and cool before mixing with the bell pepper, scallions, onion, mint, and almonds.

3. Mix together the sesame oil, vinegar, soy and chili sauces, and pepper in a small dish and adjust the amounts as desired.

4. In a large bowl, toss the dressing, edamame, and all the other ingredients until well blended. Serve.

Make the Edamame Salad into an entrée by adding salmon.

Look for items such as sesame oil and chili sauce in the international section of your grocery store. If you're able to find only frozen edamame in the shell, thaw and remove them from shells according to package directions.

sunshine soup and salad

In the spring and summer when you are always on the go, there's nothing like a light and refreshing meal to boost your energy. These fresh recipes for soups and salads are perfect warm weather meals. Pair them together for delicious combos or add them as a starter to a grilled entrée. Also try our tips for garnishing soup, as well as a tart and tangy homemade dressing to pair with your salad.

> Turn this simple soup into a main dish by omitting ½ cup of water and 1 cup of the chicken stock to create carrot-ginger puree. Serve with grilled chicken breast or seared scallops.

sunshine ginger carrot soup

What better way to celebrate extra hours of sunlight than with a cheery soup! By pairing fresh carrots with ginger, we spice up the ordinary. Plus, try some great tips for garnishing and creating a "ray of sunshine" design in the center of each bowl.

SERVES 3–4

Ingredients

- 1½ tablespoons butter
- 1½ teaspoons ground ginger
- 1 medium onion, diced
- 4 large carrots (about 1 pound), peeled and grated
- 1½ teaspoons coarse salt (or ¾ teaspoon table salt)
- 2 cups low-sodium chicken stock
- 1 cup water
- 1½ tablespoons granulated sugar
- ½ cup half-and-half (optional)
- ¼ cup sour cream or plain yogurt

Instructions

1. Melt the butter in a medium saucepan over medium heat. Add the ginger and cook until fragrant, about 15 seconds.

2. Add the onion, carrots, and salt, and stir to combine. Lower the heat to medium-low and cook for 5 minutes.

3. Add the chicken stock, water, and sugar. Bring to a simmer until the vegetables are soft, about 10 minutes. Add the half-and-half (if using).

4. Transfer the carrot mixture to a blender and cover, or use a hand blender. Blend until pureed, about 30 seconds.

5. Divide the hot soup among serving bowls and add 1 tablespoon of sour cream or yogurt in the center of each bowl. Use a toothpick to create sunrays by gently spreading the sour cream outward on the surface of the soup.

> For garnish, look for candied ginger at your local grocery store near the dried fruit or baking goods. Finely chop the ginger and use as a sweetly spiced garnish.

watermelon cucumber soup

Here is a soup that's as cool as a cucumber. Enjoy it as a light, refreshing meal in the summer months. It is also healthy, delicious, and easy to prepare.

SERVES 4

Ingredients

2 small watermelons
1 seedless cucumber
Juice of 1 lime
Zest of ½ lime
Pinch of salt
½ teaspoon olive oil
Granulated sugar to taste
Mint leaves for garnish

Instructions

1. Cut the watermelons in half. Scoop out the pink flesh and place in a blender or food processor. Save the rind halves for bowls.

2. Peel the cucumber and cut into pieces.

3. Blend the watermelons, cucumber, lime juice, lime zest, salt, olive oil, and sugar in a blender or food processor until they reach your desired texture.

4. Pour into the rind halves and garnish with the mint leaves. Serve chilled.

Pair your soup and salad meal with multigrain bread or crackers to help soak up every last drop of this wholesome goodness.

For a vibrant and flavorful garnish, chop one of your favorite fresh herbs such as parsley, chives, or tarragon, and create a ring around the edge of the soup.

crisp spring salad with citrus poppy seed dressing

There is no better companion for soup than this light and fruity salad. The fresh fruit ingredients will have you singing the praises of spring and the homemade dressing provides a bright and tart complement.

SERVES 4

Ingredients

FOR THE DRESSING

2 tablespoons fresh lemon juice (approximately ½ to 1 lemon)
¼ cup fresh lime juice (approximately 2 limes)
3 tablespoons orange juice without pulp
1½ teaspoons red wine vinegar
1 clove garlic, minced
¼ teaspoon granulated sugar
½ teaspoon salt
½ cup olive oil
½ tablespoon poppy seeds
Black pepper to taste

FOR THE SALAD

1 bag spring mix salad greens
2 ounces blue cheese (or more if desired), crumbled
1 cup whole red grapes
2 medium-ripe Anjou pears, sliced
½ cup dried cranberries
1 cup sliced unsalted almonds
Grilled chicken slices (optional)

Instructions

1. Place all the dressing ingredients in a jar with a tight lid and shake vigorously. To blend the flavors, let stand in the refrigerator for 30 minutes before serving.

2. Rinse and dry the salad greens and fresh produce.

3. Toss all the ingredients together in a large salad or serving bowl.

4. Sprinkle the desired amount of dressing over the salad and toss, or serve on the side in small bowls.

marinated beet salad

This quick and easy recipe is a great dollar-stretching dish for cooking on a budget.

SERVES 4–6

Ingredients

2 cans or jars of beets, sliced

MARINADE

2 tablespoons apple cider
2 tablespoons red wine vinegar
2 tablespoons caraway seeds
1 teaspoon granulated sugar
2 tablespoons minced Vidalia onion
1 teaspoon horseradish
¼ teaspoon ground allspice
Salt and pepper to taste
5 tablespoons olive oil

Instructions

1. Place the beets in a large bowl.

2. Prepare the marinade by combining all the ingredients.

3. Pour the marinade over the beets and let stand for several hours before serving. Stir the beets occasionally to coat evenly with the marinade.

comfort food to warm your soul

One of the first things we associate comfort with is warm homemade food. The sentiment is just as important as the food itself, and nothing feels better than making meals that your family loves. During cold months, cozy up with new recipe ideas for a rich pumpkin black bean soup and a great turkey sandwich that will show your friends and family just how much you care. They are sure to become new favorites at your table.

slow down and enjoy

Taking your time when preparing a meal for your family is one of life's simple pleasures. No matter how much pride you take in getting a meal to the table in no-time flat, making a meal that's truly memorable is so rewarding no matter how much time it takes. Treasure those occasions when time isn't your number-one priority, whether it's a big fall holiday feast or a weekend family dinner.

pumpkin black bean soup

This thick, rich soup is delicious on a chilly fall day and is a perfect accompaniment to your holiday turkey—especially if you or someone you love is a vegetarian.

SERVES 8–10

Ingredients

4 tablespoons olive or canola oil
½ cup chopped shallot or red onion
2 garlic cloves, minced
3 tablespoons ground cumin
1 teaspoon kosher salt
½ teaspoon ground pepper
1 teaspoon cinnamon
1 teaspoon allspice
3 cans (14.5 ounces) black beans, drained and rinsed
1 can (14.5 ounces) diced tomatoes
4 cups vegetable broth
1 can (16 ounces) pumpkin puree
3 tablespoons balsamic vinegar
Baked pumpkin seeds for garnish (see recipe below)

Instructions

1. Place the oil, shallot or red onion, garlic, cumin, salt, pepper, cinnamon, and allspice into a large pot and cook over low-medium heat until the shallot or red onion and garlic begin to brown.

2. Using a food processor, puree the beans and tomatoes with half of the vegetable broth. Add the pureed beans, tomatoes, pumpkin, and the rest of the broth to the pot.

3. Simmer the mixture, uncovered, until thick, about 40–45 minutes. Before serving, stir in the balsamic vinegar. Garnish with baked pumpkin seeds.

> You can add less vegetable broth to create a thicker soup and substitute a half stick of margarine for oil if preferred.

> Instead of using a food processor, use an immersion blender to simplify the process. You can puree the ingredients together inside the pot you're using to cook the soup.

baked pumpkin seeds

Garnish the soup with this tasty topping and store the extras for use as a healthy snack.

MAKES 2 CUPS

Ingredients

- 2 cups pumpkin seeds
- 2 tablespoons light cooking oil (vegetable, peanut, or other)
- 1 teaspoon spice (cayenne, garlic powder, cumin, curry, or any favorite; add more or less to taste)
- 1 teaspoon salt, if desired

Instructions

1. Preheat the oven to 350°F.

2. Dry the seeds between two paper towels if necessary.

3. Mix the spice and salt into the oil and toss the seeds in the mixture.

4. Spread the seeds on a baking sheet. Bake approximately 30 minutes or until crisp and very lightly browned. Toss occasionally. Serve as a soup garnish or snack.

homemade bread basics

Homemade foods are a great way to show your love and appreciation for others. Loaves of bread straight from your own oven make great gifts for housewarming or dinner parties and can add something special to any meal. Follow these basics whenever you bake bread, and you can't go wrong:

- Always follow instructions exactly and don't skip steps. Bread making can take time, but the end results are worth it!

- Learning to bake bread properly will make your experience more enjoyable. Set up all your ingredients and utensils on a counter or other work surface, play some relaxing music, and pour a glass of your favorite beverage.

- To streamline the process, put away and clean as you go.

- Always preheat the oven completely before putting the bread in to bake.

- Try to use fresh ingredients whenever possible.

- When handling dough, coat your hands with flour to keep it from sticking.

warm turkey and havarti sandwich

Perfect for leftover Thanksgiving turkey, this kitchen creation is served open-faced on warm homemade bread and topped with sweet and simple mango chutney.

MAKES 8 SANDWICHES

Ingredients

1 loaf homemade bread, thickly sliced (see page 104)
Nonstick olive oil spray
16 slices Havarti cheese or 1 bar of Havarti, sliced
Leftover turkey, finely sliced
Simple Mango Chutney (see page 86)

Instructions

1. Preheat a toaster oven to broil or preheat the oven to 400°F.

2. Spray the bottom of each piece of bread with a small amount of olive oil and place on a baking sheet. Lay a slice of Havarti on top of each piece.

3. Put the sheet into the toaster to broil or in the oven to bake just until the cheese melts on the bread, then remove.

4. Place the leftover turkey on top of the melted Havarti and top with a heaping spoonful of Simple Mango Chutney.

5. Top with another slice of Havarti and return the tray to the toaster oven to broil or the oven to bake just until the Havarti has melted, about 3 minutes.

6. Transfer to a plate and serve hot. Top with additional Simple Mango Chutney as desired.

> These sandwiches can be served for lunch or as hors d'oeuvres at a holiday party.

pasta smarts

Because the world of noodles can be overwhelming, we tend to limit ourselves to pasta types that are most familiar to us. If you love Italian food but are tired of spaghetti and meatballs, venture into some new pasta shapes and sauces. This quick guide will introduce you to some different types of pasta and how to prepare them. Try these simple, yet delicious recipes to start discovering new pasta dishes in your own kitchen.

pasta basics

Most pasta is made with the same basic ingredients, so you may wonder why there are so many shapes and sizes. The answer is that different pasta forms hold sauces differently. A large tubular pasta is great for thick, meaty sauces, while small elbow macaroni is best for thinner, more delicate sauces.

As you navigate the pasta aisle to choose the kind that's best for your recipe, a few helpful hints may keep you from feeling overwhelmed. Also reference our guide to pasta to familiarize yourself with some types you may never have used before.

- One type of pasta can go by several different names, such as rotelle, which is also known by its nickname, "wagon wheel pasta." If you see pasta that you thought you knew by another name, chances are it's actually the same pasta.

- The same type of pasta can come in different sizes. The name will cue you to the size. Names ending in *ini* mean "little," whereas pasta with names ending in *oni* are larger. For example, rigatoncini is a smaller version of rigatoni.

pasta guide

SHAPES	USE	STUFFED	USE
Campanelle	Delicate sauces	Cannelloni	Stuffed with cream, seafood, poultry, or vegetable sauces
Farfalle (bow ties)	Tomato sauce or pasta salad	Mandu	Can be steamed, boiled, deep-fried, or panfried
Fusilli	Rich, creamy sauces, baked dishes, pasta salad, and soup	Tortellini	Tomato or oil-based sauces

TUBULAR	USE	RIBBON	USE
Bucatini	Any sauce	Fettuccine	Creamy and oil-based sauces
Rigatoni	Tomato sauces, meat sauces, and thick creamy sauces	Lasagna	Baked dishes with tomato and meat sauces
Ziti	Thick, creamy sauces, chunky tomato sauces, and baked dishes	Linguine	Creamy tomato and oil-based sauces

ROUND-RODS	USE	Notes
Angel Hair	Delicate cream or tomato sauces	
Vermicelli	Delicate to medium sauces	
Spaghetti	Medium to thick sauces	

classic alfredo

Try this simple no-fail favorite. It is the perfect fall-back recipe when you're craving Italian but don't have a lot of time to cook.

SERVES 4

Ingredients

- 2 tablespoons butter
- 1 quart heavy cream
- 4 cups grated Parmesan cheese
- 2 teaspoons white pepper
- 1 pound dry fettuccine noodles, prepared according to package directions

Instructions

1. Place the butter and heavy cream in a saucepan over medium heat. Do not allow the mixture to boil.

2. Once the mixture cooks down by half, begin adding cheese 1 cup at a time, stirring continuously.

3. Stir in the pepper.

4. Add the pasta, toss, and serve.

> Never cook pasta the full cooking time suggested on the box. Instead, cook until it's al dente, which means "almost firm." Pasta actually continues cooking until you serve it!

whole wheat pasta with asparagus, roma tomatoes, and herbs

Experiment with different pasta shapes using this wonderfully creamy and complex-tasting recipe. Use our guide to pasta shapes to help you choose. We recommend fusilli or rigatoni, which are both excellent for heavy cream sauces like this one.

SERVES 4

Ingredients

1 pound dry whole wheat pasta of your choice
1 pound asparagus
6 tablespoons olive oil
Salt and pepper to taste
2 cups large diced Roma tomatoes
2 teaspoons minced garlic
¼ cup heavy cream
½ cup Italian dressing
¼ cup basil, cut into ¼-inch strips
¼ cup minced flat-leaf parsley
¼ cup chopped chives
½ pound pecorino cheese, freshly grated

Instructions

1. Prepare the pasta according to package directions.

2. In a bowl, coat the asparagus with 4 tablespoons of oil and sprinkle with salt and pepper.

3. Lay the asparagus on a sheet tray and broil until soft and slightly charred (approximately 10 to 15 minutes). Cut into ½-inch pieces and set aside.

4. Place the remaining olive oil in a large sauté pan and bring to medium heat.

5. Add the tomatoes, asparagus, and garlic. Cook for 2 minutes.

6. Add the pasta and toss.

7. Stir in cream and cook until it has been absorbed.

8. Add the Italian dressing and toss to coat the noodles.

9. Remove from the heat and stir in the parsley, basil, and chives.

10. Top the pasta with the cheese as you serve.

> Make this pasta dish even heartier by adding your favorite meat. Try grilled chicken, sautéed shrimp, or sliced strip steak.

southwestern pasta

This is an Italian dish with a Tex-Mex twist. The penne noodles hold this sauce perfectly for a bold and creamy burst of flavor with every bite.

SERVES 4

Ingredients

1 pound dry penne noodles
2 tablespoons vegetable oil
½ cup cream
1 or 2 chipotle peppers, minced
2 limes, juiced
½ cup minced cilantro
1 cup grated pepper jack cheese

Instructions

1. Prepare the penne according to package directions.

2. Add the vegetable oil to a large sauté pan set over medium heat.

3. Add the penne and toss to coat in the oil.

4. Stir in the cream and cook until absorbed.

5. Add the chipotle peppers and toss.

6. Add the lime juice and toss to coat.

7. Remove from the heat and toss with the cilantro and pepper jack cheese before serving.

personalize your pizza

Before you turn to takeout, look at the ingredients you have on hand and consider cooking a pizzeria-inspired dinner right at home. When you choose the ingredients, from meats and cheeses to fruits and nuts, it's as if you're cooking in your very own bistro. Begin with simple step-by-step dough recipes and then build your perfect pizza with unique flavor combinations and personalized touches.

pizza dough demystified

Take the guesswork out of your pizza preparation with this simple savory dough recipe. If you have a bread machine, you can use it as an alternative way to make this homemade dough.

quick and easy pizza dough

MAKES ONE 12-INCH PIZZA CRUST

Ingredients

1 package dry yeast
¾ cup warm water
2 cups flour
1 teaspoon salt
1 teaspoon granulated sugar

Instructions

1. Preheat the oven to 450°F.

2. Let the yeast soak in a bowl of warm water about 5 minutes.

3. Add the flour, salt, and sugar, and knead for 2 to 3 minutes to blend.

4. Cover the bowl with a lid or kitchen towel and let the mixture rise in a warm area for 15 minutes.

5. With a floured rolling pin, roll out the dough to fit a 12-inch pizza pan.

6. Bake in the oven for 10 to 12 minutes, until golden brown. Leave the oven on to bake your completed pizza later.

Running short on time? You can always pick up pre-made dough from your local grocery store.

gourmet made simple

Once you have baked your dough, it's time to pile on the ingredients. Take a cue from these fun flavor themes, adapted from the sunny Mediterranean as well as a small bistro in France.

mediterranean pizza

Ingredients

1 clove garlic
Prepared 12-inch pizza crust
2 tablespoons olive oil
4–6 ounces feta cheese, crumbled
1½ cups dry spinach leaves
½ cup halved grape tomatoes
¼ cup black olives
¼ cup banana peppers

Instructions

1. Preheat the oven to 450°F.

2. Remove the garlic clove from its skin, soften with clean fingertips, and rub generously over the entire crust.

3. Apply the olive oil, spreading it with the back of a spoon or your fingertips.

4. Top with the feta cheese, spinach, tomatoes, olives, peppers, and optional meats (see box at right).

5. Place the pizza back in the oven and cook for 5 to 7 minutes, or until the cheese is lightly browned and bubbly.

> To make this dish heartier, add 4 strips of bacon, crumbled, or 3 pieces of prosciutto (Italian ham), thinly sliced.

vegetarian bistro pizza

MAKES ONE 12-INCH PIZZA

Ingredients

4–6 ounces pizza sauce (from can or jar)
Prepared 12-inch pizza crust
4–6 ounces goat cheese, crumbled or sliced
3–5 roasted red peppers (from a jar), sliced
1 yellow bell pepper, sliced
1½ cups dry spinach leaves
2 tablespoons balsamic vinaigrette
Salt and cracked black pepper to taste

Instructions

1. Preheat the oven to 450°F.

2. With a spoon, spread an even layer of pizza sauce over the entire crust.

3. Top with the goat cheese and red and yellow peppers. Add the spinach leaves and drizzle with the balsamic vinaigrette. Sprinkle with salt and pepper to taste.

4. Place the pizza back in the oven and cook for 5 to 7 minutes, until the cheese has been lightly browned and is bubbly.

baked brie pizza

MAKES ONE 12-INCH PIZZA

Ingredients

Prepared 12-inch pizza crust
2 tablespoons butter or margarine, melted
4–6 ounces Brie, sliced
2 pears, seeded and thinly sliced
½ cup chopped walnuts

Instructions

1. Preheat the oven to 450°F.

2. Brush the entire crust evenly with melted butter or margarine.

3. Top with the Brie, pear slices, walnuts, and optional meats (see box at left).

4. Place the pizza back in the oven and cook for 5 to 7 minutes, or until the cheese has lightly browned and is bubbly.

For another topping you can also add ¼ pound roasted chicken or turkey, shredded or sliced.

something sweet

After the main course, keep the pizza party going with a heavenly Fruit and Cream Pizza Tart (page 172). The Sweetheart Pizza Dough—accented with orange juice and sugar—and fresh, colorful fruits put a surprising twist on pizza.

sweetheart pizza dough

MAKES ONE 12-INCH PIZZA CRUST

Ingredients

- 1 cup all-purpose flour
- 1½ teaspoons baking powder
- 2 tablespoons granulated sugar
- 4 tablespoons butter, softened
- ½ egg yolk
- 2 tablespoons orange juice

Instructions

1. Preheat the oven to 350°F.

2. Mix the flour, baking powder, and sugar in a medium-sized bowl.

3. Add the butter and knead the ingredients together with clean hands or in a food mixer.

4. Add the egg yolk and orange juice. Continue to knead until the ingredients form a doughy consistency.

5. Remove the dough from the bowl and wrap tightly in plastic wrap. Chill in refrigerator for at least 15 minutes.

6. Roll out the dough with a floured rolling pin and shape to fit into a 12-inch pan. Bake for 20 to 25 minutes or until golden brown.

> Instead of making the dough, you can skip a few steps by using store-bought sugar cookie dough, rolled and shaped to fit a 12-inch pan.

fruit and cream pizza tart

MAKES ONE 12-INCH PIZZA

Ingredients

- 1 cup granulated sugar
- 1 cup water
- 4–6 ounces chocolate-hazelnut spread (found in the peanut butter section of most grocery stores)
- 4–6 ounces whipped cream topping
- Prepared Sweetheart Pizza Dough, cooled (see recipe on page 171)
- 2 oranges, peeled and thinly sliced
- 2 pears, skinned, seeded, and thinly sliced
- 4 kiwis, skinned and thinly sliced

Instructions

1. Create a simple syrup by combining the sugar and water in a saucepan over medium-high heat. Bring the mixture to a boil, stirring constantly. Once the sugar has dissolved, remove the syrup from the heat and let cool.

2. As the syrup cools, spread a generous layer of chocolate-hazelnut spread and then a layer of whipped cream across the entire pizza crust.

3. After the syrup has cooled, pour it into a medium-sized bowl. Lightly toss all the fruit slices in the syrup and then arrange decoratively on the crust. Begin at the center and arrange the fruit in a fanning circular design, working your way toward the edge of the crust.

Staying in for dinner means cleaning up after yourself, but with dishwashing solutions from Dawn and Cascade you can cut through grease and stuck-on food on every pot, pan, and dish with ease.

create your own couscous

Quick-cook versions of couscous are now widely available in grocery stores and offer the perfect base for economical last-minute meals. Couscous is so versatile that it can be eaten plain or flavored, warm or cold, and as a light entrée or side dish. Plus, it offers an ideal quick fix for your weekly leftovers!

couscous basics

Couscous, which is semolina wheat pasta, is often served under a meat or vegetable stew, but it will adapt and capture any flavor combination you want to mix in. Begin by purchasing quick-cook couscous in bulk or boxed couscous that comes with a seasoning packet to keep on hand. Couscous is prepared using even parts of liquid and pasta, and the rest is up to you. Be creative!

couscous base

SERVES 4

Ingredients

> 1 cup water
> 1 teaspoon butter or margarine
> ¼ teaspoon coarse salt
> 1 cup couscous
> *or*
> 1 box of prepared couscous with a flavor packet of choice (follow package directions)

Instructions

1. Bring the water, butter or margarine, and salt to a boil and add the couscous. Remove from the heat, cover, and set aside for 4 to 5 minutes.

2. Remove the cover and fluff the couscous with a fork.

make it your own

Use these suggestions, alterations, and additions to create your own special couscous dish.

- **Add Flavor:** Although preparation calls for 1 part couscous and 1 part water, you can also use leftover broth (chicken, beef, or vegetable) or milk to enhance the flavor. After the couscous is prepared, you can add the seasoning packet, fresh herbs (parsley, mint, basil, cilantro, dill), oils, or dressings to create a bed of flavor that will complement your meal.

- **Add Veggies and Protein:** If you'd like to add produce, sauté the vegetables in 1 tablespoon of olive oil and about ½ teaspoon of salt for 2 or 3 minutes prior to adding the liquids. If you want to incorporate leftover meats, dice or pull the meat into bite-sized pieces and heat separately in a microwave or in a saucepan prior to adding the liquids.

- **Make It Breakfast:** For an easy breakfast dish, prepare couscous with milk or orange juice instead of water. Add additional flavor with brown sugar or maple syrup and top with chopped nuts, yogurt, or your favorite fruit.

simple meal suggestions

Try some of these suggestions for meal combinations. Once again this depends on what's in your pantry or refrigerator, but start with these ideas and have some fun. Think of it as building a pizza with all your favorite flavors and ingredients.

work space

Notes on couscous

mediterranean-style couscous

As a nod to the region where couscous originates, this version of the dish offers a great opportunity to use produce you have on hand, and can be served warm or cold.

SERVES 4

Ingredients

- 2 cups couscous in flavor of your choice
- 2–3 tablespoons oil-based dressing such as balsamic vinaigrette, Greek, or Italian
- 1 cup garbanzo beans (also called chickpeas)
- ½ cup chopped onion, sautéed
- ¼ cup chopped sweet pepper, any color, sautéed or roasted
- ¼ cup mild or hot banana peppers, chopped
- ¼ cup olives, sliced or chopped
- ½ cup artichoke hearts, chopped
- ½ teaspoon fresh parsley, chopped
- ½ teaspoon lemon, zest or juice
- 2 tablespoons feta or goat cheese, crumbled

Instructions

1. Prepare the couscous according to package directions.

2. Drizzle the couscous with the oil-based dressing. Add until desired consistency.

3. Add any herbs, lemon zest, or juice. Use whatever you have on hand and sounds good.

4. Now the real fun begins: Add some of the tasty ingredients mentioned above or feel free to make substitutions with ingredients you have in your fridge or pantry.

5. Toss the ingredients with the prepared couscous, place in a serving bowl, and top with crumbled cheese and chopped parsley, as desired.

couscous with a latin twist

Rethink taco night using these ingredient suggestions or other combinations of Latin flavors that you have in your kitchen.

SERVES 4

Ingredients

1 box prepared couscous with a flavor packet of choice (follow package instructions)

Salsa or Pico de Gallo

Seasonings like cumin, red pepper, or chili powder

Additional ingredients such as

Black beans, drained and rinsed

Sweet corn kernels

Sweet peppers, any color, chopped and sautéed

Onions, chopped and sautéed

Jalapeño peppers, chopped

Black olives, sliced or chopped

Mexican cheeses, shredded

Fresh cilantro, chopped

Chorizo sausage (optional)

Ground beef (optional)

Instructions

1. Drizzle the couscous with salsa or Pico de Gallo.

2. Add any seasonings you desire. Toss with additional ingredients such as those listed or what you have on hand. Transfer to a serving dish.

3. Top with any variety of Mexican cheeses and some fresh chopped cilantro, as desired.

> Don't forget to try couscous as a great cost-saving leftover lunch or even a unique cold salad for a potluck or picnic. Cooked couscous will keep in the fridge for up to three days when stored in an airtight container.

Most meat lovers can't get enough ribs, but few are brave enough to cook them at home. Contrary to popular belief, however, it's not hard to cook fall-off-the-bone ribs at home. And the best part is that once you learn the basic barbecue recipe, you can use a variety of meats and add different rubs or sauces for a unique flavor every time.

never-fail ribs

Try this recipe for delicious, tender meat. It works for both beef and pork. Once these are prepared, they're ready for your favorite barbecue sauce. If you would like to use a rub, make sure to apply the rub mixture before cooking your meat. Our selection of rub recipes below offers some great ideas.

SERVES 4

Ingredients

Rub (optional, see recipes that follow)
2 cuts (4–6 pounds) of beef or pork ribs

Instructions

1. **Preheat the oven to 275°F.**

2. **Apply the rub if using.**

3. **Cover a sheet tray well with foil. Place the ribs on the tray bone side down. Cover the ribs and sheet tray with foil.**

4. **Place the tray in the oven and bake for 5 to 5½ hours. Avoid opening the oven because it will interfere with the cooking process.**

5. **Remove the ribs from the oven, add your favorite sauce, and enjoy.**

Lining your tray with foil will take care of most of the mess. For any leftover dripping, use Dawn, which cuts through grease with ease.

savory pork rub

Onion, garlic, and paprika give this rub recipe its warm, hearty taste. It's great if you prefer rich flavor over spicy heat. This rub recipe complements pork best, but it also works well with beef and chicken.

MAKES ABOUT 2½ CUPS

Ingredients

> 1 cup paprika
> 2 tablespoons salt
> ½ cup onion powder
> 2 tablespoons ground pepper
> ¼ cup garlic powder
> ¼ cup brown sugar

Instructions

1. Mix all the ingredients in a bowl until well blended.

2. Pat the rub over the meat and follow the Never-Fail Ribs recipe (page 179) for cooking directions.

hot and tangy beef rub

For best results try this rub on baby back ribs. The deep flavor of beef stands up well to this bold rub recipe. While beef is recommended, you can also use chicken or pork.

MAKES ABOUT 2½ CUPS

Ingredients

> 1 cup light brown sugar
> 2 tablespoons salt
> ¼ cup cayenne pepper
> ¼ cup onion powder
> ¼ cup garlic powder
> 4 tablespoons dried thyme
> 2 tablespoons ground black pepper
> 2 tablespoons ground cinnamon
> ¼ cup chili powder

Instructions

1. Mix all the ingredients in a bowl until well blended.

2. Pat the rub on your meat and follow the Never-Fail Ribs recipe (page 179) for cooking instructions.

spicy chicken rub

Cumin, red pepper, and mustard give this rub recipe its bold flavor. While it was created with chicken in mind, it's also wonderful for pork and beef ribs.

MAKES ABOUT 2½ CUPS

Ingredients

- 1 cup paprika
- 2 tablespoons ground cumin
- 1 tablespoon salt
- 1 tablespoon ground black pepper
- ¼ cup chili powder
- ¼ cup brown sugar
- 1 tablespoon crushed red pepper
- 2 teaspoons mustard powder
- 4 chicken breasts

Instructions

1. Preheat the oven to 375°F.

2. Mix all the ingredients until well blended.

3. Pat the rub on chicken to give it a nice coating.

4. Place the chicken on a foil-lined sheet tray. Bake uncovered for 20 to 25 minutes.

5. Allow to cool for 5 minutes and then slice. Add your favorite sauce as you serve.

sweet barbecue sauce

Enjoy this sweet and mild flavor on any of your favorite meats. It's also tasty as an appetizer with kettle chips for dipping.

SERVES 4–6

Ingredients

2 cups ketchup
½ cup water (or for extra flavor, substitute chicken stock for chicken or beef stock for pork or beef)
½ cup apple cider vinegar
¼ cup light brown sugar
2 tablespoons Worcestershire sauce
1 tablespoon onion powder
1 tablespoon garlic powder

Instructions

1. Combine all the ingredients in a heavy saucepan.

2. Bring to a low boil, then turn down heat, and simmer for 20 minutes, stirring occasionally. The sauce should be a little thin but not watery.

3. Serve on your favorite meat or with kettle chips for dipping.

The flavor of your sauce will heighten after 24 hours in the refrigerator. When possible, make your sauce ahead for the fullest flavor. Reheat until a light steam is seen and then serve.

hot barbecue sauce

Use this spicy sauce to heat up any dish.

SERVES 4–6

Ingredients

1 tablespoon vegetable oil
1 onion, minced
3 cloves garlic, minced
1 can (16 ounces) tomato sauce
1 can (8 ounces) tomato paste
3 tablespoons dark brown sugar
2 tablespoons white vinegar
2 tablespoons crushed red pepper
2 teaspoons cayenne pepper
1 tablespoon salt
1 tablespoon crushed black pepper
½ cup water
2–3 dashes cayenne pepper sauce

Instructions

1. Put the vegetable oil in a heavy saucepan, oven medium heat.

2. Add the onion and cook until it turns golden brown.

3. Add the garlic and cook for 1 minute, stirring continuously.

4. Add the remaining ingredients and simmer about 20 minutes.
   Serve immediately or chill overnight and reheat for fullest flavor.

molasses barbecue sauce

Give any meat a deep, smoky flavor by topping it with this sauce. It is also superb on the grill.

SERVES 4–6

Ingredients

½ cup water
½ cup ketchup
¼ cup yellow mustard
¼ cup brown sugar
½ cup cider vinegar
¼ cup molasses
1 tablespoon salt
1 tablespoon ground black pepper
2 tablespoons soy sauce
½ tablespoon liquid smoke

Instructions

1. Mix all the ingredients in a heavy saucepan except the soy sauce and liquid smoke. Simmer for 20 minutes.

2. Add the soy sauce and liquid smoke, and simmer for another 10 minutes. Serve immediately or chill overnight and reheat for fullest flavor.

Liquid smoke is a sauce that helps you achieve the same flavor you get from cooking meat in a smoker. You can find it at your local grocery store in the same area as such condiments as hot sauce and ketchup.

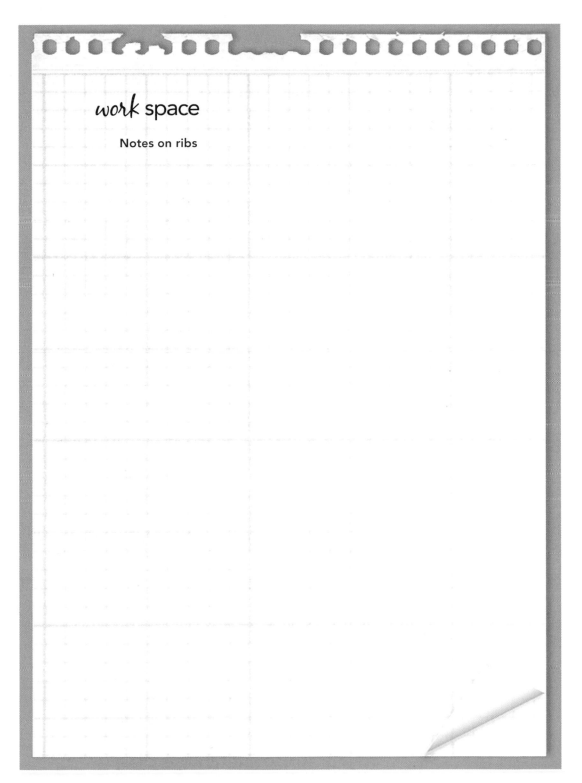

work space

Notes on ribs

deliciously meatless

Whether you are cooking for a vegetarian or just trying to cut a little meat from your diet, your family and friends are sure to love these delicious ideas. They are flavorful, hearty, and easy to recreate again and again with your favorite vegetable selections.

layered vegetable casserole

This steamy casserole gives you the flavor of comfort food without the same level of cholesterol that's associated with many meaty dishes. Instead of lasagna noodles you'll use a smart substitute: strips of eggplant! Try this recipe in the winter to warm up with family and friends.

SERVES 4–6

Ingredients

2 tablespoons olive oil
2 tablespoons garlic
2 bell peppers, diced
1 white onion, diced
2 zucchinis, diced
2 yellow squash, diced
2 carrots, grated
2 eggplants, cut lengthwise into ½-inch-thick slices
2 cups balsamic vinegar

Instructions

1. Preheat the oven to 375°F.

2. In a bowl, combine the olive oil, garlic, peppers, onion, zucchinis, squash, and carrots. Toss well and set aside.

3. Cover the bottom of a baking dish with some of the eggplant slices. Spoon some of the vegetable mixture over the eggplant.

4. Repeat the layers in step 3 until the baking dish is full.

5. Place in the oven and bake for 35 minutes.

6. Meanwhile, bring the balsamic vinegar to a boil in a saucepan and reduce to a syrup. This process should take about 20 minutes.

7. Spoon the reduced sauce over each helping of casserole.

roasted vegetable risotto salad with lemon vinaigrette

The complex savory flavors in this simple-to-make salad are sure to be a crowd pleaser. Enjoy it as a light entrée, a side dish, or a healthy vegetarian-friendly touch to any potluck spread.

SERVES 4

Ingredients

- 1 quart vegetable stock
- 6 tablespoons olive oil
- 1 white onion, diced
- 1 pound dry Arborio rice
- 4 cups grated Parmesan cheese
- 1 bell pepper, cut into ½-inch strips
- 1 red onion, cut into ½-inch strips
- 1 zucchini, diced
- 1 yellow squash, diced
- 2 teaspoons minced garlic
- ½ cup lemon juice
- 1 teaspoon white vinegar
- 1 bunch parsley, minced
- ½ cup ½-inch strips of basil leaves

Instructions

1. Preheat the oven to 375°F.

2. Bring the stock to a low boil in a medium saucepan.

3. Heat the oil in a large saucepan and sauté the white onion until golden brown.

4. Add the rice to 2 tablespoons of oil and stir constantly to brown it.

5. Add 1–2 ladles of the stock to the rice and stir constantly. Repeat until all the stock has been added.

6. Add 3 cups of Parmesan to the risotto, ½ cup at a time.

7. In a bowl, combine the bell pepper, red onion, zucchini, squash, and garlic. Toss with 3 tablespoons of olive oil to coat.

8. Place the vegetables on a foil-lined sheet tray. Roast for 15 minutes.

(continued)

Arborio is rounded medium-grained Italian rice that is traditionally used for risotto because it is firm and creamy when cooked. Look for it in the regular rice section of your local grocery store or in the international foods aisle.

Substitute the vegetables in this dish with seasonal selections for a different flavor every time you make it.

9. While the vegetables roast, make the vinaigrette by placing lemon juice and vinegar in a food processor or blender. With the motor running slowly, add 4 tablespoons of the olive oil. Set aside.

10. Combine the vegetables and rice.

11. Pour the vinaigrette over the rice and vegetables and toss well.

12. Add the parsley and basil and toss once more. Garnish with the remaining cheese and serve.

jasmine rice with soy-glazed vegetables

Try this delectable entrée for a wholesome meal made in less than an hour. It's especially perfect for spring and summer.

SERVES 4

Ingredients

4 tablespoons vegetable oil
2 cups jasmine rice
2 teaspoons minced garlic
1 quart vegetable stock
¼ pound carrots, peeled and cut at an angle into ½-inch-thick slices
¼ pound sugar snap peas
1 red bell pepper, cut into ½-inch slices
¼ pound bean sprouts
1 teaspoon crushed red pepper
½ cup soy sauce
½ cup pure maple syrup
1 bunch cilantro

If you have an avid meat lover in your bunch, broil a chicken breast until brown and cooked through (approximately 10 minutes) and then add it to that person's serving.

Instructions

1. Put the vegetable oil in a stockpot set over medium-high heat.

2. Add the jasmine rice and garlic and stir continuously for 3 to 5 minutes, until the rice starts turning golden brown.

3. Add the vegetable stock and bring to a boil. Lower the heat, cover, and simmer for 20 minutes. Remove from the heat and set aside.

4. While the rice is simmering, add the other 2 tablespoons of olive oil in a large saucepan. Bring to medium-high heat.

5. Add the carrots and sauté them for 5 to 8 minutes, until tender.

6. Add the snap peas, bell pepper, and bean sprouts. Cook for another 5 minutes, until all the vegetables are tender.

7. Add the crushed red pepper, soy sauce, and maple syrup. Stir until the sauce ingredients are combined and the vegetables are well coated.

8. Once the rice has cooked, add the cilantro and mix well.

9. Place a scoop of rice on a plate and a spoonful of vegetables on top.

sweet and simple no-bake desserts

Finishing a meal with a delicious treat can be as simple as it is sweet. All you need are a few ingredients and easy recipes like these. Try one the next time you're looking for a dessert to make ahead or something you can create when your oven is already occupied with a different dish.

quick and delicious mousse

This creamy dessert is easy to whip up and even easier to customize. Consider mousse when you're looking to please both adults' and children's tastes.

SERVES 4

Ingredients

- 1 package (8 ounces) semisweet chocolate morsels
- 1 quart heavy cream
- 1 cup powdered sugar

Instructions

1. Fill a double boiler or saucepan with water and bring to a low boil.

2. Place the chocolate morsels in the top of a double boiler. If you do not have a double boiler, place the morsels in a glass or metal bowl and place the bowl over your saucepan. Pour ¼ cup of heavy cream over the morsels and stir until they are melted and fully incorporated into the cream. Set the double boiler pan or bowl aside.

3. Place the remaining heavy cream in a bowl and whip with a mixer until it begins to thicken. Add the powdered sugar and continue beating until stiff peaks appear. Avoid overbeating.

4. Slowly fold the melted morsels into the whipped cream until mixed well.

5. Chill for 1 hour. Serve in individual dishes.

> Creating a different flavor of mousse is as easy as using different morsels. Try white chocolate or butterscotch!

grilled peaches with ice cream, honey, and mascarpone cheese

Serve the perfect hot-and-cold combo the next time you grill outside. This dish is just peachy in late summer, at the height of the fruit's season.

SERVES 4

Ingredients

2 ripe peaches
4 scoops of your favorite ice cream
4 tablespoons honey
1 package (6 ounces) mascarpone cheese

Instructions

1. Preheat the grill to medium-high.

2. Cut the peaches in half and remove the pit.

3. Place the peaches cut side down on the grill for 7 minutes. Rotate and cook on the other side for 7 minutes, until the peaches are softened and lightly charred.

4. Place each peach half on a separate plate, cut side up. Drizzle 1 tablespoon of honey over each one.

5. Place a scoop of your favorite ice cream in the center of each half and top with a dollop of mascarpone cheese. Serve immediately.

Peach season is late July through August. Seek the best at your farmers' market. Set your peaches in the window until they are fully ripe. You will know when they're ready because they'll be fragrant and give slightly to the touch.

pink grapefruit and lemonade granita

Cool, refreshing, and easy to make the night before, a granita is the perfect addition to any summer gathering. This slushy drink is sure to hit your—and your guests'—sweet spot.

SERVES 4

Ingredients

2 cups pink grapefruit juice
2 cups lemonade
1 cup sugar
Lemon wedges for garnish

Instructions

1. Mix the grapefruit juice, lemonade, and sugar together, making sure that the sugar dissolves completely.

2. Pour into a freezable container and place in the freezer until fully frozen (12 to 24 hours, depending on your freezer).

3. Once frozen, take a fork and pull across the length of the container, scraping the mixture until slushy.

4. Place in a decorative glass and add a lemon wedge for garnish.

Choose any flavor for your drink by substituting other types for the pink grapefruit juice. You may like to try raspberry, pomegranate, or strawberry juice.

Make a beautiful presentation by serving this drink in a sugar-rimmed champagne glass or a margarita glass with a lime wedge.

fresh star fruit with sugared mint

Aside from being wonderfully refreshing, this dish is as easy and as healthy as a dessert can be! Also, if you grow mint in an herb garden, this is a great way to put it to use.

SERVES 4

Ingredients

3–5 star fruit
1 cup sugar
1 bunch fresh mint
Mint leaves to garnish

Instructions

1. Cut the fruit into 1-inch cubes. Set aside.

2. Place the sugar and mint in a food processor and process until well combined.

3. Toss the fruit with the sugared mint to coat.

4. Serve in a large bowl or in individual dishes. Garnish with fresh mint.

> Vary this recipe by substituting for the star fruit any of your favorite fruits, such as strawberries, bananas, melon, or kiwi. You can even mix several for a sweet and minty fruit salad.

Yummy desserts are a great reminder that life sure is sweet. Make these to please any crowd, especially during the holiday season. With recipes this simple and scrumptious, you just might be tempted to keep a batch for yourself. Don't worry; your secret's safe with us.

crispy cinnamon sugar palmiers

Take a cue from the French and get sophisticated with these surprisingly simple caramelized pastries.

MAKES 2 DOZEN

Ingredients

Nonstick cooking spray
1 box (17.25 ounces) puff pastry, thawed
1 egg beaten with 1 tablespoon water
½ cup sugar mixed with 1 tablespoon cinnamon

Instructions

1. Preheat the oven to 400°F. Spray 2 baking sheets with the nonstick spray and set aside.

2. Unfold the pastry on a lightly floured surface, and brush with the egg mixture.

3. Sprinkle the pastry with 2 tablespoons of the cinnamon-sugar mixture.

4. Lift the 2 long edges of the pastry and gently fold them into the center.

5. Brush the dough with the egg mixture again and then sprinkle with 1 tablespoon of the cinnamon-sugar mixture. Fold the longer sides into the center again, brush the dough with the egg mixture, and top with the cinnamon-sugar.

Palmier dough can be frozen until you are ready to bake and serve. Once baked, the pastries will keep for two to three days if stored in an airtight container at room temperature.

(continued)

6. Continue the process, as though closing the pastry dough like a book, until you have created an 8-layer rectangle. Use the egg mixture and cinnamon-sugar to top the final layer.

7. Repeat the above steps with the second piece of thawed pastry.

8. Cut each dough rectangle into 12 equal squares. Place each one on your baking sheets, approximately 2 inches apart.

9. Top each piece with the remaining egg mixture and cinnamon-sugar.

10. Bake the palmiers for 12 minutes or until golden brown. Cool on a wire rack and then serve.

apricot pine nut shortbread diamonds

Make a few simple ingredients shine with this tasty twist on a classic confection.

Ingredients

½ cup (1 stick) butter, softened
2 teaspoons almond extract
¼ cup sugar
¼ teaspoon salt
1 cup flour
¼ cup cornstarch
½ cup apricot preserves
½ cup pine nuts

Instructions

1. Preheat the oven to 350°F. With an electric mixer, combine the butter, almond extract, sugar, and salt until creamy and well blended.

2. Add the flour and cornstarch and then mix again until well blended.

3. Remove the dough from the mixing bowl and press evenly into an 8-inch-square baking pan.

4. Pierce the dough all over with a fork. Spread the apricot preserves across the dough and then sprinkle with the pine nuts.

5. Bake for 25 to 30 minutes, or until the dough is golden brown and the preserves are bubbling. Let cool in the pan on a wire rack for at least 20 minutes.

6. While still in the pan, use a small, sharp knife to carefully cut the cooled shortbread into diamond or square shapes. Place them in mini-muffin papers and serve.

Add dimension and whimsy to your dessert presentation with stackable cake stands and footed trays. Get eclectic by browsing local flea markets and vintage shops for one-of-a-kind pieces.

ganache-glazed brownie bars

One word: heavenly. Soft, rich brownies and warm chocolate ganache make these bars a must-have.

MAKES 64 PIECES

Make your shortbread diamonds and brownie bars far ahead of time. They'll stay fresh in the freezer for thirty days in a sealed airtight container.

Ingredients

Nonstick cooking spray
4 ounces unsweetened chocolate
1 cup (2 sticks) unsalted butter
2 cups sugar
2 teaspoons vanilla extract
4 eggs
¼ teaspoon salt
1 cup flour
Chocolate Ganache (recipe follows)

Instructions

1. Preheat the oven to 350° F. Line a 9" × 13" baking dish with aluminum foil. Spray with nonstick cooking spray.

2. Place the chocolate and butter in a large microwave-safe bowl and heat for 2 minutes or until the butter is fully melted. Remove from the microwave and stir until the chocolate is melted and the mixture is smooth.

3. Stir the sugar into the chocolate-butter mixture until fully incorporated. Add the vanilla extract and eggs, one at a time, stirring well after each addition.

4. Stir the salt into the flour and then add the flour slowly, in small amounts, stirring until the mixture is uniform.

5. Pour the batter into the prepared pan and smooth the top with the back of a spoon. Bake for 25 minutes or until an inserted toothpick comes out clean. Allow the brownies to cool completely. Remove the aluminum foil to lift the cooled brownies from the baking pan, and frost generously with Chocolate Ganache.

6. Cut the frosted brownies in half and then in half again to create 4 equal rectangles. Cut each rectangle in half to create 8 equal pieces and then cut each piece into 8 smaller bars to create 64 brownies. Place the brownies in mini-muffin papers and serve.

chocolate ganache

FROSTS 64 PIECES

Ingredients

1 cup heavy cream
8 ounces semisweet chocolate chips

Instructions

1. Pour the heavy cream into a microwave-safe container and heat on full power for 1½ to 2 minutes, or until very hot.

2. Place the chocolate chips in the bowl of a food processor or blender and chop finely.

3. As the motor runs, pour the hot cream through the feed tube and process until the chocolate is melted and smooth.

4. Let the mixture stand at room temperature until thick and glossy but still spreadable.

5. If not using the ganache right away, refrigerate it in a covered dish until ready to frost your brownie bars.

> Ganache can be made three days ahead and chilled in a covered dish. Be sure to let it stand at room temperature for two to three hours to soften before frosting your brownies.

outside pleasures

plant. grow. *nurture.*

The natural world can revive your surroundings and add a refreshing dimension to your home, both inside and out. Whether you have a green thumb or not, there are plenty of creative ways you can garden, decorate, and enhance your home with the help of nature's bounty.

Step outside your home and think about all the possibilities. Your porch, patio, and garden offer many opportunities for making your home even more beautiful. The plants, flowers, and seasonal surprises found outdoors might even make the perfect addition to your home décor.

In the pages that follow you will find simple advice for livening up your outside spaces and bringing the outdoors in. We encourage you to get the family involved, try something new, and watch your garden grow, wherever it may be.

six steps to finding a house plant for you

House plants can be the perfect way to bring nature into your home. They can often prove to be more difficult than people expect, however, which is why it's important to pick the type of plant that fits best with your home and your habits. Whether this is your first house plant or you're looking to add a new one to your collection, this simple guide will help you choose a plant that is sure to flourish in your unique home conditions.

1. find your plant style

Your first step toward finding the perfect house plant is to decide exactly what your plant style is. Think about the look and feel of your home. Understanding the look you have and what plant fits in with that style will help you narrow your choices.

Would you call your home décor "classic," or does it seem a little more contemporary? For a more classic look you may like symmetrical, full, leafy plants such as ferns. For a more contemporary look you may want to choose something more organically shaped, such as a jade or spider plant. Is your style colorful or monochromatic? For color, look to flowering plants. To fit a monochromatic color palette, consider something of various shades of green, maybe with stripes or spots.

2. no-grows

Before introducing a new plant into your home, always check with the store representative or the National Poison Center to find out whether the plant is safe if accidentally ingested by a child or a pet. If you choose to grow potentially toxic plants, be sure to keep them out of reach. Just to be safe, you may want to avoid growing them altogether.

3. fuss factor

Choosing a plant that fits your lifestyle will ensure that it stays healthy, happy, and beautiful for you to admire. While some require frequent feeding and watering, some do not. Some plants need a partial drying-out period between watering; others do not. If you tend to embrace routines, you may like a plant that you water a little each day or every other day, such as impatiens. If not, you may like a plant that requires a very minimal, irregular watering pattern, such as a cactus. Either way, be sure to familiarize yourself with how much care a plant will need before deciding if it's right for you.

4. go high or low?

Start thinking about where you would like your house plant to live. Are you looking for a touch of green for your kitchen counter or the desk in your home office? Will it fill an empty corner in a large room? Or are you looking for something that hangs overhead? Understanding the space you're hoping to fill will help narrow your options.

5. window of opportunity

It can be frustrating to watch a plant weaken or die because the light conditions aren't optimal in your home for that particular plant type. Instead of choosing a plant before a spot, try finding the spot and then picking a plant that works best there. Here are some ideas for how to do that.

Once you have chosen a location for your new house plant, determine the spot's lighting conditions. To do this you will need to ask yourself a few questions:

- **How close will the plant be to the window?** Will the plant be flush against glass, or will it be several feet away?

- **Which way does the window face in relation to the sun?** If it faces to the south, you'll get the most direct sun. If the window faces east or west, the plant will get partial direct sun. Otherwise, consider the area anywhere from bright but sunless to shady.

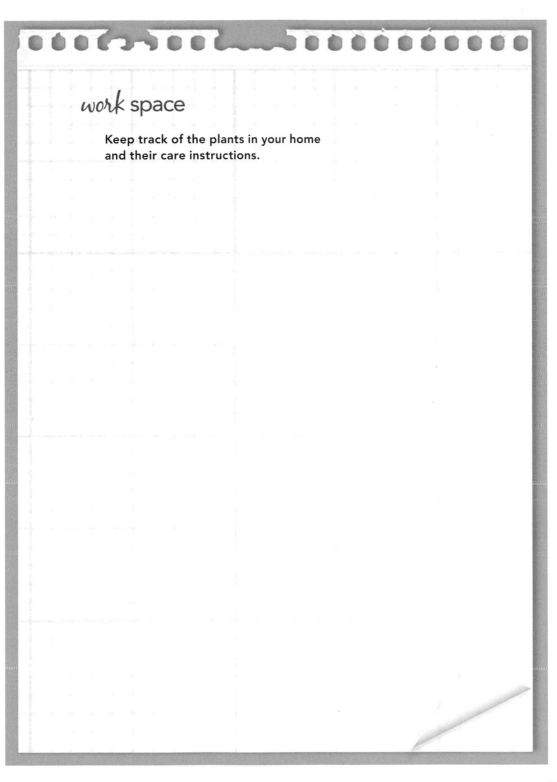

work space

Keep track of the plants in your home and their care instructions.

- **How direct will the sunlight shine?** Will the light be diffused by window coverings or any other obstructions inside your home? Similarly, is there anything outside that will block light, such as a tree or large shrub? If so, this window does not provide direct sun.

Based on your answers, would you consider this spot to have a low, medium, or high amount of light overall?

6. pick a plant

Now it is time to consider all the decisions you made in steps one through five. Together, your answers should give you a good idea of your perfect house plant. Now you just have to find one. Here is a guide filled with suggestions to help you begin your search. You can also share your style and conditions with a knowledgeable staff member at your local nursery who can give you additional recommendations.

guide to house plants

		☀	⛅	☁
Hanging	💧	Jelly Bean Plant	Spider Plant	
	💧💧	Wax Plant	Asparagus Fern	Boston Fern
	💧💧💧	Prayer Plant	Arrowhead Vine	Christmas Cactus
Table	💧	Mother-in-Laws Pillow	Any Succulent	Impatiens
	💧💧	Jade Plant	False Aralia	Coleus
	💧💧💧	Aloe Vera	Scarlet Star	Aglaonema
Floor	💧	Yucca	Dumb Cane	
	💧💧	Mother-in-Laws Tongue	Peace Lily	Boston Fern
	💧💧💧	Urn Plant	Swiss Cheese Plant	Herringbone Plant

breathe easy at home

Bringing plants into your home can add natural beauty and a bright splash of color, but did you know they can actually improve your air quality, too? Research has shown that certain types of plants can remove toxins and pollutants commonly found in homes today. Check out this vibrant collection of common household plants that also clean the air. Then try our tips for displaying your leafy beauties and keeping them healthy.

breathe easy

Certain plants act as natural "indoor air scrubbers" that can substantially improve the air quality inside your home. Going far beyond simply producing fresh oxygen, many indoor plants can also filter such toxins as benzene and formaldehyde. These toxins often exist in our indoor environment because they're used to make numerous household materials.

Plants are highly efficient at absorbing chemicals in the air through microscopic openings in their leaves. Once these plants absorb the bad stuff, they either break down the chemical or send it to their root system where it is released into the soil and broken down.

plants for healthy air

Many plants can help purify the air, but researchers have found that the following common household plants are air-filtering all-stars. Also see Six Steps to Finding a House Plant for You on page 205 for more house plant ideas.

flowering

Chrysanthemum (Pot Mum)

Gerbera Daisy

Peace Lily

> If you have an average 200-square-foot living room with 8- to 9-foot ceilings, two to three medium-sized plants will make a great contribution to improving the air quality. For other rooms try using one plant per 100 square feet.

green leafy plants

Bamboo or Reed Palm	Golden Pothos
Chinese Evergreen	Janet Craig
Corn Plant	Marginata
English Ivy	Warneckii

display your plants

Plants can be a colorful complement to your home décor. Try these tips for displaying them throughout your home:

- Tall, stately plants such as bamboo palm and corn plant can create a dramatic look in the corner of a room potted in a large planter. Give the display a modern, natural flair by setting small pots of golden pothos at the base of the tall plants to fill out the bottom.

- Create a Zen-like indoor rock garden by covering the bottom of a waterproof tray with smooth, round pebbles. Cover the pebbles with water and place a few potted plants on top.

- Use a chrome or brass kitchen hanging basket to display plants that sprout flowing runners such as golden pothos and English ivy.

- Make a colorful tiled base for flowering plants such as pot mum, peace lily, and gerbera daisy. Set a plastic mat on the surface where you'd like to display your flowers and arrange patterned or solid-colored ceramic tiles over the mat. Experiment with different floral arrangements and sizes, and change them with the seasons.

- Window boxes can be a beautiful addition inside, too. Place clusters of plants inside a decorative window box and set it on a shelf, mantel, or hall table to bring the natural look of the outdoors inside your home.

> Light requirements for indoor plants vary widely by type, and not all of them need to be displayed in front of a window. Check your plant care tag for specific instructions.

care for your plants

Read the care tag that comes with your plant for guidance on specific light, temperature, soil, and watering recommendations. Also keep these tips in mind to ensure that your plants are healthy and working at their peak air-cleaning condition:

- Some plants don't need as much water as others, so be careful not to overwater. As a general rule, water a plant if it feels dry an inch or more into the soil depth.

- Using a pot with drainage holes in the bottom will help you avoid overwatering. Stop watering when water flows from the drainage hole and into the collection saucer. Pour out the excess water from the saucer.

- Cold tap water can be a shock to your plants' roots, so use room-temperature water.

- In the winter, adjust your watering schedule to account for drier conditions when the furnace is running.

- Good potting soil is your best option for healthy indoor plants. While your garden soil may look rich and vital, it might have bacteria, insects, or fungus that could harm your plants.

With a little tender loving care, these lively plants can be amazing helpers for keeping the air in your home clean and healthy for years to come.

the basics of landscape design

Many times it is not the most beautiful house on a street that stands out. It is the one with the most thoughtfully designed and cared-for lawn. Amazingly, it is not always the work of a professional landscaper or gardener. You, too, can put your yard to work beautifying your home. All you need are the same basic design principles that professionals use and some fundamental knowledge about common plants. Follow these guidelines, and you'll be set to design your own landscaping.

breaking down design basics

The great part of landscaping is that it's never permanent. Instead, it is an ever-evolving work of art that changes every season and matures every year. No matter what your style may be, some general design principles apply to all landscaping. Keep these in mind as you create, transform, or tweak your yard's design.

- **Simplicity:** This design principle applies as much to landscaping as it does to the visual arts. There are lots of beautiful options out there and, as hard as it may be, try to limit your color and plant palettes. Choosing and staying with a simple scheme will help your lawn feel cohesive and will complement your home.

- **Balance:** This principle is important for keeping a sense of equality among the elements in your yard. By having a balanced design the space feels whole and complete. There are a couple of ways to accomplish balance. Symmetry is a little more formal and centers around the idea that one side of your yard is a reflection of the other's plant shapes, sizes, and colors. Asymmetrical balance is a little more organic. You can vary plant types and placement more freely as long as there is a sense of equal visual weight throughout the yard.

- **Unity:** Using elements consistently throughout your design will create a sense of harmony. You can achieve this by repeating a certain

> To test your yard's balance, stand back from your home. If your eye is continually drawn to a certain area or plant, it means the design is out of balance. Bring it back to balance with the tips given here.

plant or color in many places, either clustering them or dispersing them evenly throughout the yard. This common item will tie all the others together. Pick two or three colors and one or two plants for repeating. You'll be amazed how they create a visual rhythm that really finishes off the look of your landscape.

- **Texture:** Texture creates depth for your landscaping. Try more coarse-textured plants with more variegated colors in the foreground and softer, solid-colored plants in the background.

- **Color:** Color is the finishing touch for your landscape. These are the touches of interest that really catch the eye of passersby. Bright colors pop out at you, while cool colors recede and draw you in. For ideas about how to design your yard so that it is always in bloom, see Always in Bloom on page 225.

maintain a motif

Sometimes creating a landscape design is easier if you have a theme. It helps you maintain harmony by narrowing your plant and color options. Here are just a few ideas to help you start thinking about what your motif can be. Consider the architecture and style of your home as you choose your theme.

- **Pruned and Pretty:** This is a more formal, classic, and orderly motif featuring symmetrical patterns and straight lines. Look for more traditional geometrically shaped plants and well-pruned shrubs. This look is perfect for historic homes such as those with traditional redbrick architecture, columns, or cobblestones. This is also a great motif if you take a lot of pride in your yard and enjoy the upkeep.

- **Cool and Casual:** This motif is contemporary and asymmetrical. The plant placement is seemingly random, and the color scheme may be monochromatic for a sleek finish. Try this look if you have contemporary or modern architecture. It is a great low-maintenance option for families.

- **Gorgeous English Garden:** This is a wonderfully colorful and complex look. Other than some anchor elements such as shrubs and trees, this idea features beds overflowing with flowers. Because the flower beds seem to have a little bit of everything, there is always something new to notice. Try incorporating garden features such as a bench, archway, or birdbath. This is good for Cape Cod–style homes or anything with a cozy cottage feel. While this theme looks carefree, it actually involves the most plants, gardening knowledge, and time.

- **Whimsically Woodsy:** This motif is natural and seemingly organic. You can mimic the way that plants grow in nature by letting them grow naturally rather than pruning them to look perfectly symmetrical. Focus on a woodland color palette, such as browns and greens. Try this for craftsman-style homes, bungalows, log cabins, or homes with a lot of natural wood detail. This is a great motif for families because it is easier to maintain than others. If something is a little out of balance or overgrown, no one will ever notice!

know your yard

Before choosing the plants for your design, check out these practical considerations. The best landscape designs fit your yard's conditions and your personal lifestyle. This series of questions will help you decide what types of plants will work best for you.

- **Conditions:** First and foremost, consider your conditions. Is your yard very sunny or mostly shady? Maybe it is some of both. Also, is the dirt dry or moist? For a beautifully flourishing yard, choose plants that match your conditions.

- **Maintenance:** Do you enjoy caring for your yard, or do you need a low-maintenance design that doesn't require time-consuming pruning and watering? Choose plants that synch best with your lifestyle.

- **Uses:** Who will be enjoying your yard, and how? Is this design to showcase your home from the curb, or do you have children or pets to consider? For children and pets, choose hardy, durable plants that won't get damaged if they're handled or brushed up against. Also consider avoiding plants with thorns.

plan, then plant

It is a good idea to sketch your landscape, in order to bring your vision one step closer to reality before you start shopping and planting. Try to have a good understanding of what you need and where you'll position everything. This will help you estimate your costs more easily. You will also avoid buying extras you thought you had space for or being left with gaps after you plant. Plus, it's fun!

example bubble diagram

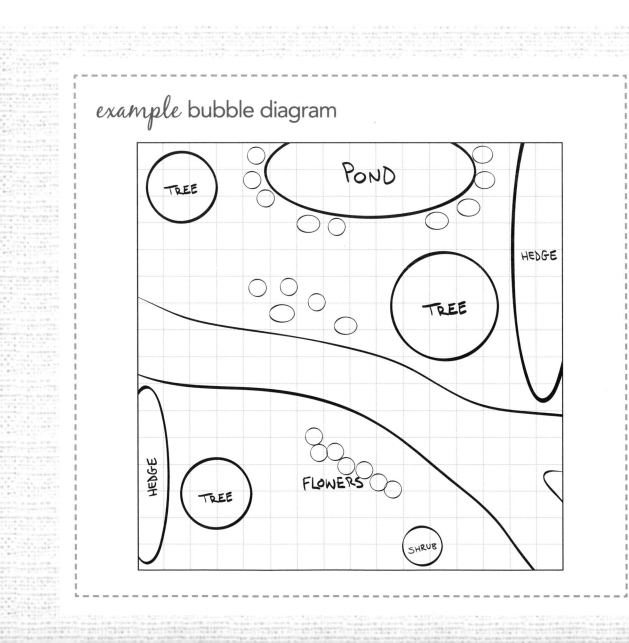

work space

Design your landscaping by creating a bubble diagram here. Simply mark off where your house and walkways are, and fill around them with "bubbles" representing the size and placement of each plant.

the facts on fertilizer

From banana peels and leftover salad to raked leaves and grass clippings, it is easy to repurpose your own household waste—both indoors and out—into valuable fertilizer or eco-friendly compost. Begin by learning the basics of compost creation and discover the ideal location for composting in your own home. Sprawling yard or not, it is easy to transform your waste into nutritious material for our planet—and your garden will reap the benefits, too.

compost done right

Holidays such as Earth Day and Arbor Day are the perfect times to kick off your own compost system, but you can start one any time you'd like. Cleaner air, richer soil, and taller plants are only a few steps away. But to properly prep your new fertilizing system, first take this quick course on compost fundamentals.

what is compost?

Used as a soil conditioner and fertilizer, compost consists of the remnants of organic matter that are naturally decomposed by microorganisms. Organic matter such as leaves, grass, and "green" kitchen waste, such as fruits and vegetables, are ideal for creating rich compost. Because such items typically make up 20 to 30 percent of a household's total waste, composting prevents these materials from taking up precious space in your local landfill.

how does compost work?

Consider compost the secret weapon of every good gardener. When placed in your garden or plant container, compost returns organic material to the soil, thereby loosening heavy clay soils for better root penetration, improving the soil's capacity to hold water and nutrients, and stimulating the growth of beneficial microorganisms. The result? Stronger and larger plants for you to enjoy. In addition to their beautiful blooms, healthy plants clean our air and conserve our soil.

how do I make compost?

Your job when making compost is to provide the optimum environment for the beneficial microorganisms to do their work. In ideal conditions the decomposition process works very quickly—often in as little as two weeks.

1. **Layer upon Layer:** Start your pile with a layer of "green" materials. This includes green leaves, grass clippings, and organic, nonmeat kitchen scraps. Compost no-no's include any animal material, such as meat scraps, bones, dairy products, grease, and pet waste. Your second layer should contain "brown" materials, such as garden soil, brown leaves, and straw. Wet these two layers and add another layer of green materials. Finally, top off your pile with a touch of garden soil.

2. **Turn and Turn:** It is important to continue your composting by actively managing your pile. Turn your mound occasionally, gradually shifting the materials closer and closer to the center where they can heat up and decompose. Also add water periodically to keep the mound moist. When it is ready to use as garden fertilizer, your pile will be black, crumbly, and sweet-smelling.

where do I stow my compost?

Although compost can be strewn around your yard in piles, it is best to stow the material in a sturdy well-ventilated bin that protects the compost against extreme temperatures and inclement weather. You can purchase a compost bin at your local hardware store or garden center, but first consider using everyday materials and a bit of elbow grease to craft one with ease.

- **Concrete Blocks:** Use four stacks of concrete blocks to create a supportive structure for your compost pile. For better aeration, stagger the block towers. You can even use acrylic paints to decorate the stones in a way that complements your home's exterior and garden.

- **Wire Mesh Bin:** Using galvanized chicken wire or hardware cloth and a heavy-duty staple gun, create a simple circular bin. Because it

> Turn your compost creation into a family affair by assigning each family member a different layer and designating one person as "compost manager," responsible for overseeing production of the pile.

doesn't have posts, the bin is easy to lift and provides quick access to finished compost at the bottom of the pile.

- **Garbage Can Bin:** Take a heavy-duty plastic garbage can, 30 gallons or larger, and drill small holes around the entire can, top to bottom, approximately 3 inches apart. This project is perfect for repurposing old garbage cans that have developed holes or tears in the plastic.

how do I use my composting bin?

Once you have selected your bin, create 3- to 4-inch-thick layers of your materials, alternating between carbon-rich and nitrogen-rich items until the bin is full.

Rule of (green) thumb: Composting doesn't need to be an exact science. Regardless of how it is organized, all organic matter breaks down eventually. If you have more brown materials than green, don't fret. Your compost will simply break down at a slower rate, and you can always add more green items as they collect.

> **Be sure to place your bin in a sheltered area, such as along the side of your garage, where it is well protected from direct sunlight and strong winds.**

think outside the bin

If outdoor space is an issue, try forgoing the traditional compost bin and create your own nutrient-rich fertilizer with an everyday plastic garbage bag. Simply fill a garbage bag with dried leaves and twigs and add two to three scoops of garden soil and a heaping handful of dry granular fertilizer. Add water to slightly dampen the mixture, seal the filled bag, and place it in a sunny location. Consider your back patio or balcony or outside where your garbage receptacles are stowed. Let the bag sit for several months. When you open it, you'll find an abundant supply of rich, ready-to-use compost.

a community effort

If your home lacks green space or you'd prefer not to keep a bin at home, you can still partake in the composting process through your neighborhood's organizations. With local gardens and public recycling services available in most areas, even the most space-restricted urbanites can compost their organic waste.

- **Community Gardens:** Put your green thumb to work. Learn to landscape like a pro and make wonderful friends along the way. When you become involved in a community garden club, you typically gain access to the group's communal compost bin. Donate your waste to the bin and take the fertilized material as desired to enrich your potted plants at home.

- **Farmers' Markets:** In many cities, farmers' markets provide drop-off bins for organic scraps that are used later to produce compost. Contact the establishment to see if the service is available in your area.

> Can't find a garden in your area? Contact your local Cooperative Extension System office or government office to inquire about initiating a community garden project.

unique wildflower planters

Once spring has sprung, make your neighbors green with envy: Instead of using garden-variety planters to house your blooms, make a creative statement all your own with truly special wildflower planters. These un-expected blossom displays are perfect in the yard or perched on a patio or porch and will make your home the most lively, colorful spot on the block.

Wildflowers are vibrant, hardy plants that grow quickly and don't re-quire much attention once planted. This makes them ideal for honing your green thumb or training a beginner.

You can place plants directly in a flower or mulch bed using a little top-soil and fertilizer, but consider using visually striking items such as an old sink, antique tub, basin, or wooden barrel. Brimming with vintage charm, these displays will add a touch of whimsy outside your home and spark conversation at your next outdoor get-together.

Follow these simple instructions (opposite) for filling a rustic barrel with flowers and then let your imagination run wild and try the technique on other potential planters.

> The large-scale look of an antique tub or barrel lends a dramatic effect to your garden, but consider creating pint-size versions of these displays with a collection of old-fashioned teakettles or a tin watering can.

choosing wildflower varieties

To achieve the look of flowers spilling into your garden, focus on creating dimension by planting the tallest flowers in the back of the barrel and smaller pieces in the foreground. Use the size chart below as a guide. As you plant, remember that the arrangement should look soft and organic. Work with the natural bend of your flowers and let them lie as they may.

tallest wildflowers (up to 3–4 feet)

Morning Glory

Red Poppy

Rocket Larkspur

Rose Mallow

medium-height wildflowers (up to 2 feet)

Baby Snapdragon/Toadflax

Black-eyed Susan

Cornflower/Bachelor's Button

Zinnia

shortest wildflowers (up to 1 foot)

African Daisy

Baby Blue Eyes

California Bluebell

California Poppy

wildflower barrel planter

Materials

Wooden barrel (check your local home improvement store or landscape supplier)

2 bags potting or topsoil, or enough to fill the barrel

Spade-tip shovel

Flower bed fertilizer

Wildflower seed packets

Instructions

1. Choose your planting area and then use the spade-tip shovel to dig a hole that matches the size of the barrel base. It should be deep enough so that the barrel can be partially inserted in the ground.

2. Nestle the barrel into the soil at a 45-degree angle, packing the loose dirt around the barrel base to hold it firmly in place.

3. Fill the barrel with topsoil at an angle and then scatter the remaining topsoil around the base, as though the soil is spilling out into your garden. Be careful not to fill the barrel completely.

4. Apply the fertilizer to the topsoil, following the instructions on the package.

5. Plant your wildflower seeds according to the instructions on the package. Remember to plant some in the barrel and some in your flower bed around the barrel.

your own hanging garden

The Hanging Gardens of Babylon were considered one of the Seven Wonders of the Ancient World, so it's no surprise that many home gardeners use vines, cascading flowers, and hanging baskets to create their own hanging gardens. This stunning gardening method is an easy way to add beauty to your porch or balcony—and it couldn't be easier to achieve.

Start your hanging basket indoors and then move it outside when the weather gets warmer. The plants chosen for this project should work in most climates, but ask a representative at your local gardening store what would work best in your area.

For whichever plants you use, plant your basket with two green vines for every flowering plant. This is a simple way to ensure that your basket has plenty of depth, texture, and color.

always in bloom

Only gardeners seem to know the secret for keeping their yard in bloom all year. But while it seems like quite a challenge, it is actually not as hard as you may think. With a little knowledge and planning, you can be on your way to a more beautifully blooming yard. We'll tell you how to choose the right combination of plants and how to blend them into your existing landscaping so that you, too, can enjoy colorful flowers in all seasons.

blooms from the beginning

Plant selection is the key to keeping your yard flowering. That's because each type of flower has a different blooming pattern. Some flower in the spring, while some bloom in the fall. By choosing plants according to their bloom time, you can have at least one for every month of the season. This way you are sure to have a flower or two to admire. Before purchasing any plants, you will learn to create a plan for what you have and what you need.

> When possible, perennials are a great choice because you can count on them to grow bigger and bloom more beautifully every year for many years.

month-by-month planting

The first step is to take an inventory of your current landscape. Start with the flowers you already have as well as any flowering shrubs and trees and then fill in your work space on page 229. Ask yourself, "During which months are these plants most beautiful?" Mark each plant next to the month it tends to bloom in your work space. Is there a lot of overlapping? Are there many "gaps" of time where nothing blooms? The next step is to fill in what is missing.

picking plants

Once you have determined where you already have plants blooming in your yard and when they peak, it's much easier to decide which plants you should purchase in the future. Consider this a working plan. You don't have to buy all these plants now. You can try buying one per season for a few years, or you can ask for one as a gift for a special occasion, such as your birthday.

Look over the monthly guide to flowers that follows for inspiration. It lists three flowers that require full sun, partial sun, or shade for each month of the year. This helps you to find plants for the month you need and the growing conditions you have in your space. Just remember that this is a general guide. Bloom time for each plant can vary depending on which zone you live in as well as unique growing conditions each year.

There are eleven hardiness zones. A representative at your local nursery or lawn and garden store will be happy to help you find out which zones you're in and how that affects the plants you're considering.

plant placement

Placement is important because you want balance for your blooms. You can start mapping where your flowers will go even if you don't have them all yet. Think of it as a fireworks display. You want your plants to "explode" artfully around your yard, not all in one spot at one time.

To accomplish a balanced yard of blooms, try alternating your plants. For example, place a March and an April plant opposite each other—like at two ends of your front yard, for example—equally spaced from your front door. Since two plants often overlap in bloom time, you're likely to have flowers at both ends of your yard at once. As each bloom fades away, another will begin the next month, creating a beautiful display of blooms that never ends.

create a container garden in the air

To create your own hanging garden basket, use a wire basket and sphagnum moss. This will allow you to plant right into the side of the basket. Doing so allows more plants to get sunlight and creates a basket that's completely covered in greens and flowers.

This hanging basket mixes intriguing vines, such as green and white periwinkle and the chartreuse potato, with beautiful flowers that come in many colors and shapes.

Another unique aspect of the hanging garden is that it dangles at eye level—not above your head. You can appreciate the plants blooming out of the top of the basket as much as the ones hanging below.

Materials

Wire hanging basket
Sphagnum moss
Craft knife
Newspaper
Potting soil
Oregano

Impatiens
Petunias
Periwinkle vine
Potato vine
Geraniums
Chain and hook

Instructions

1. Line the bottom of the wire basket with the sphagnum moss. On top of that layer of moss place a layer of newspaper to hold the potting soil.

2. Fill the basket ¾ full with potting soil. By the time everything is planted, the soil will reach the top of the basket.

3. Place the basket on a raised work surface, such as an overturned flowerpot, so you can work around the sides.

4. Use your craft knife to cut small slits through the moss and newspaper. They should be large enough to fit the root balls of the oregano and impatiens through to the soil inside the basket. Go all the way around the basket, cutting slits 2 to 3 inches apart. Plant two oreganos for each impatiens.

5. Plant the petunias, periwinkles, and potato vine in the soil around the edge of the top of the basket.

6. Plant the geraniums in the middle of the basket.

7. When the weather is warm enough, hang your basket from your porch or balcony ceiling with a piece of chain long enough to put it at eye level.

month-by-month guide to flowers

	☀	⛅	☁
January	Primrose Jasmine	Glory of the Snow	Christmas Rose
February	Daffodil	Star Magnolia	Candytuft
March	Bugleweed	Tulip	Milkwort
April	Iris	Pansy	Forget Me Not
May	Hydrangea	Daylily	Bleeding Heart
June	Allum	Lupine	Foxglove
July	Lily of the Nile	Dahlia	Impatiens
August	Phlox	Petunia	Hosta
September	Firebush	Creeping Daisy	Japanese Anemone
October	Pink Dawn	Confederate Rose	Hardy Begonia
November	Chrysanthemum	Mexican Bush Sage	Phontinia
December	Witch Hazel	Camellia	Cyclamen

work space

Keep your working "inventory" of plants here. You can also use it as a wish list, marking off plants you'd really love to have as you get them.

Bloom Time	Plant	Care Notes
☐ January		
☐ February		
☐ March		
☐ April		
☐ May		
☐ June		
☐ July		
☐ August		
☐ September		
☐ October		
☐ November		
☐ December		

patio, sweet patio

Do you use your deck or patio as often as you'd like? If not, try these four steps to create an outdoor living space that you'll love. With a few simple changes, your backyard will be more comfortable, cozy, and hopefully your new favorite place to entertain!

step one: it's all in the arrangement

Start by thinking about your outdoor space as being more like your indoor space. Now rethink your patio furniture arrangement.

- **Conversational Pieces:** Think about outdoor seating the same way that you think about indoor seating. Group the benches and chairs in configurations where they face one another. This makes conversation more natural between you and the people you're spending time with.

- **A Place for Everything:** Just as your sofa has an end table on which to set drinks and snacks, you also want end tables for your outdoor space. For seating options other than your dining set, be sure to have side tables nearby.

- **Serving Success:** Being able to serve food effectively is also an important consideration. Allow plenty of room for large platters, supplies (such as extra napkins), and condiments. If your patio dining set is not large enough to serve from, try a card table with a festive tablecloth for a serving station or buffet table. It will keep your tabletop less crowded and make room for more delicious food to be enjoyed. You may even want to keep a card table accessible to your outdoor space in the warm months. Store it in your garage or a closet near the closest door to your deck or patio. If you can find an inexpensive cart on wheels, even better!

- **Room with a View:** Consider what makes your patio or deck unique to other areas of your home. Most of the decorating is already done for you: Wonderful greenery, flowers, and beautiful skies are all there

and ready for you to take in. All you have to do is arrange your space so that you can really make the most of the natural setting. Surround your seating with plants. This will create a "room" and bring plant life into the conversation circle.

- **Invite Wildlife Closer:** Hang bird feeders nearby or plant flowers that are known to attract butterflies.

- **Beyond the Patio:** Look for a sturdy tree where you can hang a hammock for yourself or a swing for little ones.

step two: material matters

To withstand the elements, patio furniture is constructed of more durable materials than indoor furniture. This can make it seem harder and more utilitarian. Soften the feel of your outdoor décor by adding soft textures such as fabric. Here are some ideas for creating a cozier feeling.

- **Soft Seats:** Add a soft touch to your dining set seats with cloth chair cushions.

- **Fine Fabrics:** Cover the table with a linen tablecloth. If you have an umbrella in the center of your table, use linen place mats instead. Also look for some inexpensive cloth napkins that feature fun summer patterns.

- **Delightful Dishware:** Serve meals on your indoor plates, complete with your usual glassware and silverware, so that the space feels even more like home. Plus, the real stuff doesn't blow away!

step three: light the way

Lighting at night is key to creating an inviting ambiance. Try these tips to set your outdoor space aglow.

- **Illuminate Large Areas:** Stake tiki torches around the yard for a lot of light without a lot of cost. They are also great for creating a tropical feeling in your space.

- **Bye, Bye, Bugs:** Candles that repel insects are a great choice for illuminating an intimate space such as your table.

- **Hello, Soft Light:** While hanging lanterns do not provide a lot of light, they are the perfect way to create mood from overhead. Try stringing three to five from one end of the space to the other. Small battery-operated LED lights are available so that you don't have to coordinate electrical cords. Both the lanterns and lights are inexpensive additions to your outdoor space that allow you to use it and reuse it year after year.

step four: make it home

Once you have transformed your space, try it out! Grill this delicious dinner with family and friends and watch the sun go down for a beautiful evening that just can't be replicated indoors.

grilled crab legs with garlic tarragon butter

> To thaw frozen crab legs, place them in a deep pan (to collect water) and pull plastic wrap tightly over the top. Thaw in the refrigerator for one day. Once thawed, drain the water and wipe the crab legs dry before brushing with olive oil.

Ingredients

GARLIC TARRAGON BUTTER

½ cup (1 stick) butter
1 clove garlic, minced
1 teaspoon lemon juice
2 teaspoons dried tarragon
Cracked pepper to taste

GRILLED CRAB LEGS

2–4 pounds frozen king crab legs, thawed
2 tablespoons extra-virgin olive oil

Instructions

1. Melt the butter with the minced garlic in a small saucepan. Once the butter is fully melted, add the lemon juice, tarragon, and pepper. Keep at a simmer until the crab legs are ready.

2. Heat a grill to medium-high. Brush both sides of each crab leg with olive oil, place on the heated grill, and grill for 4 to 5 minutes, turning once.

3. Serve with individual sides of the Garlic Tarragon Butter for dipping.

> Provide guests with shell crackers to open the legs and with forks or seafood pickers to remove the crabmeat.

fresh fruit kebabs

Keep with the finger-food theme and grill fresh fruit kebabs featuring your favorite flavors of the season. You can even offer a variety of fruit choices and let everyone create their own kebabs. Try such fruits as pineapple, mango, papaya, nectarines, kiwi, and strawberries.

To grill, thread the fruit onto metal or bamboo skewers and brush with a light mixture of lemon juice and honey. Grill the kebabs over medium-high heat for 5 to 6 minutes or until the fruit is slightly browned and softened. Heating helps intensify the sweetness and flavor of the fruit. Enjoy these kebabs straight off the grill!

Soak the bamboo skewers in water for 20 minutes to prevent burning.

garden from your back door

A large garden bed can be a time-consuming challenge. So instead of planting a whole vegetable garden, simply grow herbs in planters right on your back porch. Use these tips to grow herbs in the summer and preserve them in the fall. Soon you'll discover that your small potted garden can flavor your dishes all year long!

how to buy herbs

Choose the herbs in your garden based on the flavors you like best. What herbs do you cook with most frequently? Which herbs do you really enjoy and hope to cook with more often? Once you have a list of five to ten plants, you're ready to visit your local nursery and make your selections. Choose only the largest, most healthy-looking seedlings. Consider some of these common, hardy herbs:

Basil	Oregano
Cilantro	Parsley
Dill	Rosemary
Jalapeño peppers	Sage
Mint	Thyme

pick your pots

Choose the planters where your herbs will grow. Repurposing extra planters will work perfectly, or you can purchase decorative containers that will show off your potted garden. If you are repurposing a collection of terra-cotta pots, consider painting them with chalkboard paint so you can mark each one with the name of the plant that is growing inside. Chalkboard paint works like regular paint but leaves a chalkboard surface when dried that you can write on. It can be found at your local craft or hardware store.

Create visual interest by choosing pots of different shapes and sizes, ranging from 6 inches in circumference and up. You can dedicate single pots for each plant, but since they don't require much room, consider planting several herbs together in a larger pot. This is great for growing several of the same plants, such as jalapeño peppers, or different varieties of the same herb, like sweet basil and spicy basil.

Once you have potted your plants, cluster the containers together in the sunniest spot on your patio. With minimal time and trouble you can have a complete herb garden without even picking up a shovel!

planting thyme (and more)

Plant your herbs in the spring, anytime after the last frost. Consider using potting soil with fertilizer beads for bigger, more beautiful plants. After planting, most herbs require very similar care. Give them as much morning sunshine as possible and water them as needed to keep the soil slightly moist through the growing season. If you like, you can also give them vegetable garden plant food as directed by the manufacturer. Other than that, you can snip your herbs fresh as needed for cooking.

> **Make sure your pots are set up to drain well. If you happen to have a container without a drainage hole, fill the bottom with rocks before adding the dirt and plant.**

harvest the flavor

At the end of the summer, save your leftover herbs and preserve them for use through the winter. All you have to do is bake them on a cookie sheet or hang them to dry out. With these tips you can learn how to preserve each herb and lock in the flavor as much as possible.

basil

1. Cut at the base of the stems. Wash and dry, and then strip the leaves.

2. Preheat the oven to 250°F. Spread the leaves on a cookie sheet. Place in the oven for 10 minutes and then turn the oven off and let the herbs dry inside for 40 more minutes.

3. Remove from the oven and crumble into an airtight container. Store in a cool, dark place for six months to a year.

oregano

1. Gather a bunch and cut at the base. Wash and dry.

2. Hang upside down in a dark, dry environment for about two weeks. Consider clipping the herbs to a clothesline with clothespins for easy hanging.

3. Crumble into an airtight container. Store in a cool, dark place for three to six months.

parsley

1. Gather a bunch and cut below the leaves. Wash and dry.

2. Preheat the oven to 250°F. Spread the leaves on a cookie sheet and place in the oven for 6 minutes. Turn the oven off and let the herbs dry inside the oven for 50 more minutes.

3. Remove from the oven and crumble into an airtight container. Store in a cool, dark place for six months to a year.

rosemary

1. Clip the stems at the base. Wash and dry. Strip off the sprigs.

2. Preheat the oven to 275°F. Spread the sprigs on a cookie sheet. Place in the oven for 12 minutes. Turn the oven off and let the herbs dry inside for 50 more minutes.

3. Remove from the oven and crumble into an airtight container. Store in a cool, dark place for six months to a year.

thyme

1. Gather a bunch and cut at the base. Wash and dry.

2. Hang upside down in a dark, dry environment for about two weeks. Consider clipping the herbs to a clothesline with clothespins for easy hanging.

3. Crumble into an airtight container. Store in a cool, dark place for three to six months.

transforming kitchen extras into backyard treasures

When the season lets you spend more time on your porch or in your yard, consider complementing the natural beauty of your home's outdoor landscape with a few handmade décor touches. By using cleverly repurposed glass bottles or charming kitchen-inspired wind chimes, you can transform ordinary household items into inexpensive yet beautiful displays that are perfect for adorning your outside space.

glass bottle yard décor

Right side up, bottles hold your favorite beverage or cooking oil. Upside down, they become outdoor décor! Instead of purchasing expensive ornamentation for your lawn or patio, create your own light-catching—and eye-catching—yard sculptures with glass bottles and stakes. Play with shape, size, and color to achieve a unique arrangement that you can call your own.

form and function

In addition to looking beautiful, consider the other purposes that your glass bottle arrangement can serve outdoors:

- Separate a flower bed from the rest of the yard with a border of bottles.
- Organize a garden into sections with color-coded rows.
- Create visual interest by adding clusters of colored bottles in fenced corners.
- Integrate your sculpture with tall ornamental grasses or bushes.
- Mix smaller, more ornate bottles with flowers in window boxes or pots.

bottle selection

Once function has been decided, explore the various types of bottles you can use for your new outdoor décor:

- Save your wine bottles. You'll have a classic range of deep green, brown, and burgundy colors. Remove labels by soaking the bottles in warm water for at least thirty minutes. Add a little dish liquid to help break down the glue residue.

- Craft stores often carry brightly colored bottles in reds, oranges, and bright blues. These will provide a bolder, more contemporary color palette or can be mixed in with more subdued colors to add "pop."

- Antique apothecary bottles, which always feature unique shapes and ornate fixtures, can be found at yard sales, thrift stores, and antique shops.

- Repurpose old soda bottles from the 1960s and 1970s. They're both playful and nostalgic.

- For a more eclectic mix of bottle shapes, use elegant food containers such as upscale-brand olive oil bottles, pesto jars, or jam jars.

placement

Once you have chosen your glass theme, you'll need to find the appropriate way to secure them in the ground or planter:

- Use plastic or wooden plant stakes or even metal tent stakes for bottles you'd like to arrange close to the ground.

- For taller placement, use longer poles such as tomato stakes.

- For small bottles in planters, try pieces of sturdy wire such as a coat hanger.

> **In more confined spaces use smaller objects such as antique perfume or pill bottles. They are a common and inexpensive find at antique shops.**

kitchenware wind chime

Give your old, mismatched silverware and outdated gadgets new life as a wind chime that looks and sounds beautiful.

chimes

Begin by gathering five to seven pieces of mismatched flatware, whether it's lying around your home or picked up from a dollar, thrift, or antique store. For a vintage effect look for pieces with a silver tarnish or keep things shiny with silver-plated or stainless steel knives, forks, and spoons that will reflect the sun's light.

hanger

You can use a range of kitchen items to hang your flatware, including these:

- a colorful enamel colander or grater
- an old-fashioned eggbeater with the handle facing up
- a large whisk, facing down
- a large fork with the tines curled in all directions. You can use needle-nosed pliers to bend the tines.

assembly

Use fishing line, which is weatherproof, malleable, and virtually invisible from a few feet away. Loop your line around each flatware handle and tie securely. Fasten each of the utensils to your hanger in a circular pattern, with a spoon dangling in the center as a pendulum. Hang outdoors on a lamppost or flower basket hanger.

A larger serving fork makes the perfect hanger for your culinary wind chime. With a pair of needle-nosed pliers, pull the fork tines away from each other, curling each one to create a small hook for hanging.

This eclectic, culinary-themed wind chime is the perfect gift for a friend who loves to cook.

soak it all in

You work hard to turn April showers into May flowers, so why let your blooms wilt in dry July? When spring turns to summer, make the most of your gardening efforts with these time- and cost-efficient watering tips. They will quench your plants' thirst during the hot sunny months and help keep your garden healthy all summer long.

gorgeous gardens

Regular watering can keep a garden looking fresh in the summer, but it can be a costly and lengthy task. Luckily, with these simple tips, you can conserve water, save time, and keep your garden looking great.

- **Water less often.** Not only will it save you time and water, but it can be better for your plants, too. For most fruits and vegetables, thoroughly soak the soil with about half an inch of water every three or four days. This minimizes the water lost to evaporation and encourages roots to reach farther into the ground to absorb extra moisture, making them deeper, stronger, and less vulnerable to drying out.

- **Go straight to the roots.** Save water by creating a simple drip irrigation system. This is essentially a hose full of tiny holes that delivers moisture to your plants at a slow, steady rate, giving roots time to absorb more water. Some systems can be set to run on an automated timer, which makes them almost effortless.

- **Use more mulch.** Mulch conserves water and can be a real lifesaver for plants. A 3-inch layer will act like a protective coating of the ground, holding in moisture longer so that you won't need to water as often.

> Early morning is the best time to water. It gives plants more time to absorb the water before the midday sun dries the soil. Watering overnight can make your plants damp and more vulnerable to slugs and fungi.

perfectly potted plants

Gardens aren't just in the ground. Keep your potted plants growing green this summer with these tips for watering both indoor and outdoor container plants:

- **A Good Balance:** Plants in containers can dry out quickly, but it's also easy to overwater. For a healthy house plant, choose a pot with holes in the bottom to allow the excess liquid to drain out and water whenever the topsoil feels dry.

- **Bottoms Up:** Plants absorb water most efficiently through their roots. For best results, place a potted plant with a drainage hole in the bottom inside a larger pot partially filled with water. That way, the liquid from the larger pot will slowly soak up through the soil of the smaller one, watering the roots from the bottom up.

- **Adding Moss:** Hanging baskets look lovely, but they can dry out quickly. Try lining yours with sphagnum moss to keep the water in. Available at most garden stores, it can look beautiful draping down from a wire basket.

To find the perfect house plants for you, see Six Steps to Finding a House Plant for You on page 205.

sweet succulents

Succulents are plants that store water in their leaves, stems, and roots, making them a perfect water-saving summer plant. Many are known for their exotic leaves and brilliant colors, so they can be an exciting addition to your home or garden. Here are three popular types that are beautiful, low maintenance, and completely comfortable indoors or out:

- **Cacti:** They are the most popular of the succulents—and with good reason. There are hundreds of varieties in different sizes and colors, and many produce stunning flowers. They require little water, love sunlight, and respond well to potting. Some varieties are hardier than others, so be sure to choose a cactus that adapts well to the temperatures in your area.

- **Aloe:** With its dramatic red, coral, yellow, or orange tubular flow-ers, aloe is among the most gorgeous succulents. It is low mainte-

nance and grows well in containers, making it a perfect addition to your home or garden. There are more than 450 species of aloe, and some, such as aloe vera, possess medicinal value.

- **Yucca:** Known for its beautiful flowers and spiky leaves that resemble the top of a pineapple, yuccas are found all across North America, from the Caribbean to Canada. These succulents love bright sunlight and dry weather, making them an ideal summer plant. And with more than fifty different species, ranging in size from small ground rosettes to full-size trees, there is sure to be one that is right for your garden.

a welcoming touch for your front door

It is easy to spruce up your outdoor décor with an inviting, personalized welcome mat. You'll need just a few simple supplies and these step-by-step instructions. Get some fresh air and limit your mess by completing the project outside.

choose your mat

Each of these welcome mat ideas uses a different type of base material. Both are made of a thick, durable fiber, perfect for personalization *and* cleaning off muddy shoes.

- **Woven Sisal Doormat:** Sisal is a woven fiber that comes from a cactus plant. This particular mat has a wide, square weave, ideal for working in ribbon or attaching accents.

- **Coir Doormat:** Coir is a fiber found between the husks of a coconut and has a fuzzy yet very tough, durable surface that absorbs paint well.

woven sisal welcome mat

Materials

1 woven sisal doormat
1 or 2 spools of 1-inch ribbon
Hot glue and/or floral wire

Hot glue gun
Accents that will lie mostly flat, such as
artificial flowers, leaves, or berries

Instructions

1. Purchase an inexpensive but sturdy woven sisal mat at your local home and garden store. It will most likely be medium to dark brown in color.

2. Make sure the ribbon you choose is durable enough to withstand the elements but not so bulky that it won't fit through the holes. Start by weaving the ribbon in and out, all the way around the outer edge of the mat. You can weave just once around or several times for a thicker border. Also try alternating colors to create a vibrant pattern.

3. Use hot glue or floral wire to attach your accents securely to the mat. Be sure to leave space in the center for your family or visitors to wipe their messy shoes.

By using ribbon and floral wire you can change the color of the ribbon or the accents easily for different seasons, holidays, and special occasions.

painted coir welcome mat

These instructions provide you with the basics, but feel free to try your own ideas as well. You can experiment with color or other decorative techniques such as taping off a lattice pattern on the mat, creating a border, or using picture stencils as accents.

Materials

- 1 coir doormat
- Cardboard
- 2-inch masking tape
- 1-inch masking tape
- Paper
- At least 1 can (12 ounces) enamel spray paint (choose a color that contrasts with the color of the mat)
- Card stock (for lettering)
- Scissors
- T-pins
- Ruler

Instructions

1. Lay the doormat on a flat surface outside. You can place cardboard under the mat to prevent overspray from getting on the surface.

2. Use 2-inch masking tape on the edge of the mat (flush to the edge). Use 1-inch tape to form a border ½ inch from the 2-inch tape. You can tape farther away for a thicker border.

3. Tape down paper in the center of the mat to prevent spray paint from getting into this section. Using a circular motion, spray in the border. Remove the paper from the center.

4. For a welcome message, house number, or last name, create your own stencils by tracing or printing out characters on card stock or thick paper and then cutting them out. If you need a little help with this, you can usually find letter and number stencils at the hardware store.

5. Using the T-pins and a ruler, tack down the letters or numbers on the center of the mat.

6. Using a circular motion, spray the paint over the mat. Use multiple coats for added coverage.

7. Wait 1 hour for the paint to dry before removing the tape, T-pins, and characters.

When you use stencils and spray paint, applying the right amount of paint is key to getting a great end result. Apply small amounts and reapply in layers to help prevent excess paint from seeping under the stencil.

brilliantly preserved leaves

Whether it is spring, summer, or fall, take some time to explore the outdoors. While you take your stroll, choose a few varieties of colorful leaves
to preserve and elegantly display in your home. Learn how to preserve
with two simple techniques that will help you keep your foliage looking
brilliant instead of turning brown and crumbly.

glycerin leaf preservation

Glycerin is a liquid that you're likely to find at your local drugstore. Beyond its soothing medicinal uses, it's also great for keeping colorful leaves from drying out, so you can create beautiful seasonal displays. This technique does require a bit of experimentation; some leaves simply don't react well with glycerin. Collect a variety just in case.

Materials

Colorful leaves with stems still attached
Liquid glycerin
Water
Flat pan or glass baking dish

Pebbles or other weighted items
Surfactant (also called spreader sticker, available at gardening stores and online)
Paper towels

Instructions

1. Look for healthy leaves with vibrant colors that don't appear to be damaged by frost, bugs, or disease. Be sure the leaf stems are still attached when you collect them.

2. Mix the glycerin and water inside the pan so that it is 1 part glycerin and 2 parts water. You only need enough to submerge the leaves.

3. Add 3 to 4 drops of the surfactant to the solution. This breaks down the glycerin molecules and allows it to penetrate the leaves more easily.

4. Place the leaves in the solution. If the leaves tend to float to the surface, put pebbles or weights on them to keep them submerged.

5. The leaves should remain submerged for 2 to 6 days. Keep them in a dry location, away from children and pets. Check on the leaves periodically to make sure their color is not changing drastically, although they will darken slightly. Remove any leaves that don't appear to be reacting well (that is, if they are spotting or have drastic changes in color).

6. Remove the finished leaves from the solution and dry gently with a paper towel. They should feel soft and pliable and will stay this way for months to come.

silica leaf preservation

This clever leaf preservation technique uses silica to dry the leaves while allowing them to keep their color and shape. Follow up the silica treatment with a dried flower coating or a clear spray-on glaze to help enhance and protect the dried leaves from breakage and fading in the future.

Materials

Silica gel (available at craft stores)
Microwave-safe container
Colorful leaves with short stems
1 glass of water (microwave safe)

Small paintbrush (optional)
Dried flower coating or clear spray-on glaze
 (available at craft stores)

Instructions

1. Pour the silica gel into the container to cover the bottom, about 1-inch deep.

2. If the leaves have long stems, cut them to about 1½ inches and space them out on top of the silica layer.

3. Slowly pour more silica gel on the surface of the leaves, until they are completely covered with a generous layer.

4. Place the uncovered container in the microwave with the glass of water. Microwave on medium power for 1-minute intervals until the leaves are dry. It will take 2 to 3 minutes.

5. To remove the dried leaves, slowly pour off the silica gel into another container until they are uncovered. Using your fingers or a paintbrush, gently brush off any silica that has settled.

6. To strengthen and protect the dried leaves further, cover with a layer of dried flower coating or spray-on glaze. If you are using a spray glaze, be sure to use it in a well-ventilated area and follow the package directions.

Silica gel is typically a mix of white and blue
crystals. Store it in an airtight container that is
out of reach of children and pets.

elegant display possibilities

Put your final pieces on display and experience natural colors indoors throughout the season and beyond.

> Once you have mastered these drying techniques, give them a try with flowers and other plant life you would like to enjoy longer.

- **Sweet and Simple:** Mount leaves on handmade paper with delicate straight pins inside a shadowbox-style frame. Add a handwritten botanical inscription below each leaf and display on a wall, shelf, or mantel.

- **Fun and Layered:** Show off your creativity by creating a natural collage. Mount preserved leaves on a pretty patterned background. Choose something simple that will set off the leaves and really make them stand out. Place the finished collage inside a frame and display on a tabletop or hang several collages together on a wall.

go green for the holidays

While creating your holiday home, think of festive greens beyond your holiday tree. Using this seasonal element adds rustic, elegant detail to your décor as well as the scent of fresh evergreen. Give traditional items such as ornaments and small gifts a playful twist with natural or even artificial greenery by trying out these fun, oh-so-simple projects.

embellished photo ornament

Spruce up your photographs in an instant using metal tins, greenery, and whimsical odds and ends like buttons and ribbon to create decorative ornaments. For this project stick to artificial garlands to ensure that your creations will last for years and years. They are easy to use and readily available at your local craft store.

Materials

Kitchen knife
2¼" × 3" Styrofoam egg (makes 2–3 ornaments)
Hot glue gun, set to low heat
2¼" × ¾" metal tin

Photograph, trimmed to 2 inches round
Scissors
One 9-inch piece of artificial mini garland
Embellishments (small strips of ribbon, beads, buttons, charms, and bells)

Instructions

1. With a kitchen knife cut a ¾-inch-thick piece from the larger end of the Styrofoam egg.

2. Using your hot glue gun, apply a generous amount of glue to the interior base of the tin.

3. Place the Styrofoam piece inside the tin, making sure it is firmly pressed into the hot glue and is level with the top of the tin. If the Styrofoam peeks over the top of the tin, press gently on the piece until it is approximately even.

4. Select a photograph and crop and trim it with scissors until it is 2 inches round and fits on top of the Styrofoam piece.

5. Use the glue gun to attach the photograph to the Styrofoam and then let it cool.

6. Beginning at the top center of the tin, use the glue gun to fasten the garland along the entire edge of the tin. You should have about 3 inches of garland left.

7. Use the remaining garland to make a small loop and attach it to the tin at the base of the loop.

8. Embellish your photo ornament using the glue gun.

Small metal tins are often used for votive candles or as homemade soap molds. To find one, check the soap- or candle-making section of your local craft store.

In addition to creating beautiful tree ornaments, you can hang these charming creations on doorknobs and on the backs of chairs. Try using them as gift tags or as table place cards at your next gathering.

knit mitten ornaments

Make the most of old or outgrown mittens with these adorable, inexpensive holiday decorations. Incorporating greenery, berries, and twigs lends an organic, festive touch to these darling creations. And with so many ways to liven up your forgotten gloves, you can hang one in every room of your home!

Materials

Mittens

Fiber filler (a small handful per mitten)

Mixed greens (try different varieties like Fir, Taxus, Thuja and Boxwood)

Floral wire

Berries (live or artificial "pip" berries)

Small twigs (live or artificial)

Ribbon

Three 5/8-inch (or larger) jingle bells

Hot glue gun

Small beads, buttons, and charms

Three small candy canes

Instructions

1. Lightly stuff the bottom of the mitten with fiber filler. Don't forget the thumb! Set aside.

2. Arrange the mixed greens in proportion to the mitten's size, setting the tallest pieces in the back and the shortest in the front.

3. Hold the arrangement tightly at the cuff of the mitten and use a 6- or 7-inch piece of floral wire to wrap the greens together. Begin at the base of the greens and work upward.

4. Use the excess wire to create a loop of 4 to 6 inches. Fasten the loose end of wire at the base of the loop to create a hanger.

5. Wrap the wired stems with a small amount of fiber filler as cushioning in the mitten. Insert the greens into the mitten and fluff to arrange.

6. Using small pieces of floral wire, fasten assorted berries and twigs to your greenery to add color and texture. If using pip berries, wrap the stems around your finger and then pull for a whimsical curl.

7. Attach a complementary ribbon around the mitten cuff and string on a jingle bell. Tie the additional bells onto the two ribbon ends, staggering their placement for extra charm.

8. Using your hot glue gun, attach buttons, beads, and charms to the mitten cuff.

9. Finally, insert the candy canes. Find the perfect spot to hang your mitten—which can be your tree, the doorknob of your guest bath, or even a kitchen cabinet.

Mittens for little hands work perfectly for this project, but so do socks for little feet! Dig up those long-lost children's socks, especially pairs in fun holiday patterns. They look extra sweet hung along a mantel as miniature stockings.

Never heard of pip berries? They're small, artificial berries that come in a variety of shapes, colors, and sizes, and are readily available at your local craft store. Try the small individual berries with malleable stems that you can curl for a quirky, artistic touch.

easy décor

adorn. makeover. *make yours.*

Think of your home as a blank canvas. It's ready and waiting to become a true reflection of your own unique vision, style, and personality. No matter how clean and organized your home may be, it's the meaningful personal touches that truly make it home.

Don't be afraid to think for yourself! When it comes to trends and home décor in general, remember to use what you love, what you're drawn to, and what truly represents you. Trust your instincts, and you're sure to create the home you love to live in.

We hope you feel inspired by the do-it-yourself decorating ideas in these pages and use them as your starting point. Whether you aim to make your home elegant, classic, or daring, above all else, make it your own.

perfect paint jobs

While painting a room seems simple enough, a few problems are sure to arise along the way. Keeping a toolbox of clever tips and tricks on hand can help keep your wall-to-wall makeover on track. From unexpected cracks and endless paint finishes to temperamental wallpaper that just won't budge, we have quick and simple solutions for lots of your painting predicaments.

assess your walls

Before you begin painting, it is important to examine your walls closely so that you are prepared for any obstacles you might encounter. First, consider your current color. If it's a deep, saturated hue that will be replaced by a lighter shade, begin your painting with the application of a paint primer. It will cover your dark shade with a light base, making your new hue lighter and brighter.

Next, run your eyes and hands along the walls, seeking any large holes or cracks. In addition, look for hairline fractures, which often run all the way from the floor to the ceiling. Marking each spot with a pencil will significantly speed up your repair process. If you have wallpaper, test the material before you start by peeling a small amount away from the wall at the seam. The more it gives, the easier your removal process will be.

clear the area

Once you are ready to get to work, remove your switch plates and outlet covers, and move all your furniture to the center of the room. If you are painting your ceiling or are concerned about paint splattering, cover your furniture with drop cloths or old blankets and towels. Spread drop cloths along the base of the wall you are working on to protect your floors. With your wall problems accounted for and your space properly prepped, let the wall revival begin.

pretty patches

While it can look daunting, patching holes and loose or saggy sections of drywall is actually a simple job that requires few materials.

Materials

- Utility knife
- Tape measure
- Drywall sheet (enough to fit areas to be replaced)
- Putty knife
- Quick-drying wall putty
- Fine sandpaper

Instructions

1. With a utility knife, cut the hole in your wall into a square. Measure the square with the tape measure and then cut a piece of new drywall to the same size.

2. With a putty knife, apply a light coat of wall putty around the edges of the newly cut drywall piece.

3. Place the piece in the hole in the wall, squeezing out any excess putty with the knife. Let dry overnight.

4. Once the putty is dry, use the knife to spread a thin layer of putty all over the patched area. Let dry overnight.

5. Use the fine sandpaper to sand away excess dried putty. Once smooth, paint the area with primer and then in your color of choice.

To repair a hairline crack, use plaster paste. Push it deep into the crack with your putty knife and then wipe away the excess. Let dry and sand to a smooth finish.

so long, wallpaper

However pesky your wallpaper, our easy approach uses fabric softener, a putty knife, and an able pair of hands to get your walls paper-free.

Materials
Fabric softener
Warm water
Large spray bottle
Putty knife

Instructions
1. Combine two parts fabric softener and one part warm water in a spray bottle. Starting at a wall corner or seam intersection, liberally spray a section of wallpaper and let soak for approximately 15 minutes. As you wait, begin spraying adjacent sections.

2. Return to the first sprayed area. Slide your putty knife beneath the edge of the wallpaper and begin moving the knife up and down to release the paper from the wall. Use your fingers to peel back the paper as you go, removing it in sections.

3. Once all the wallpaper has been removed, use the putty knife to lift any remaining scraps of paper. Then wipe down the walls with a damp sponge to remove any excess glue.

4. Let the wall dry for a few days and then apply a primer before painting.

Wallpaper paste can contain pesticides, so be sure to wear rubber gloves while working or wash your hands thoroughly afterward.

a fine finish

When you are ready to paint, consider the wide array of finishes available before you purchase any can of color. From matte mixes that hide your wall's flaws to high-gloss finishes that add a little glitz, there is a paint finish that will make the perfect statement in your space.

- **Matte Finish:** A flat, muted finish that is ideal for camouflaging bumps and blemishes on walls.

- **Flat Enamel Finish:** Similar to a matte finish but a more durable, rub-resistant formula that can stand up to cleaning, making it perfect for bathrooms and high-traffic hallways.

- **Eggshell Finish:** Semi-durable with just a hint of gloss, it's a happy medium between a matte and glossy finish.

- **Satin Finish:** A thick, smooth formula that offers glossy sheen, a deep, velvety texture, and high durability against cleaning and light scrubbing.

- **Semigloss Finish:** The slight luster of a gloss but with a texture that masks wall imperfections and stands up to tough cleaning; great for kids' bedrooms, rec rooms, and kitchens.

- **Glossy Finish:** Shiny, highly durable, and a bit dramatic, this finish isn't commonly used on walls but lends a bold look to cabinets, drawers, furniture, and trim.

> **For uneven walls with lots of blemishes, steer clear of finishes containing gloss. Their sheen catches the light and showcases the flaws, so use a flat finish instead.**

work space

Keep track of your home paint colors here. You can even dab paint in the sample column below, so you have a swatch to reference if the manufacturer discontinues the color.

Sample	Name	Brand	Finish

empowering colors

When your home and your mood are in need of a pick-me-up, use empowering colors to help bring a fresh perspective and renewed energy to your surroundings. One of the easiest and most effective ways to jump-start your can-do spirit is by using certain color families such as red, purple, yellow, and orange. Learn the meanings of these vibrant colors along with simple ways to incorporate them into key areas of your home. For more tips on adding color to your home, read Color Made Simple on page 53.

intensify your workouts

Red is an intense color that is associated with power, strength, courage, and high energy. With the ability to boost metabolism and raise respiration rates, red accents in your exercise room can help kick your workouts into high gear.

Use some of these ideas to add shades of red (including pink) to your exercise room:

- Add equipment such as pink hand weights and exercise balls and red yoga mats and blocks.

- Stack burgundy towels in a corner or on a shelf. Place a few red or hot pink sports bottles next to them.

- Use pushpins to mount posters, banners, or pennants that use crimson colors.

- Use accent rugs with rich shades of red.

- Paint the wall that faces you when you're on the treadmill, stationary bike, or weight bench a deep or strong shade of red.

- Hang artwork on the walls using red or pink frames or use artwork that incorporates these colors.

enliven your eating areas

A tasteful mix of yellow and orange is the perfect color combination for a cheerful kitchen or dining room that exudes happy, positive vibes. Yellow and orange are warm colors associated with fresh fruits and vegetables, health, energy, and the promise of a bright sunny day.

Use these perky colors to accent your eating areas:

- Fill a decorative bowl with clementines or lemons and use it as a centerpiece on your dining room or kitchen table. Complement it with a rich red-orange table runner or light citrus-orange place mats.

- Keep a bright yellow or deep orange teakettle on your stovetop.

- Small accents can make a big impact, so look for ways to incorporate shades of yellow and orange with cookie jars, soap dispensers, storage canisters, spoon holders, blenders, toasters, and trash cans.

- Fill a large yellow coffee mug with burnt orange napkins and place it on your kitchen table or island.

- Place a vase with fresh seasonal flowers in shades of yellow and orange on your table or windowsill.

boost your brain power

Rich shades of purple, violet, and lavender have a surprisingly strong effect on our ability to think and therefore achieve. Purple is associated with wisdom, memory, imagination, creativity, and strategic problem solving—making it a smart choice for accents in your home office or study.

Boost your brain power with a few of these decorating ideas:

- Add purple folders, notepads, a mouse pad, lamp, or stress ball to your desk or surrounding work area.

- Hang inspirational messages in purple frames on the walls.

- Mount a wall clock with purple accents.

- Paint a steel file cabinet, wooden bookshelf, or wall shelf a rich violet and use lavender vases as bookends.

- Hang a map using a purple frame to remind yourself that the world is full of adventure and potential. Use purple pushpins to mark the places you've been or the places you want to go.

artfully arranged artwork

Grouping artwork of different sizes and shapes can seem daunting, but when done right, these displays can add beauty, color, and intrigue to your home décor. Before you put holes in the walls, take an artistic moment to arrange your frames in a unified composition that packs some serious design punch.

get comfortable

Start with a room that has all the furniture in place before you decide where your art is going to go. Lean your artwork against the wall or place it right on the ground, and then let it rest for a while. You'll get the chance to pass by it again and again, getting a sense of how it meshes with the space's existing décor. Continue to examine it. Once you decide if your artwork has found the right room, begin to play with some different, easy-to-do compositions.

a single line

For a hallway or long stretch of wall, put frames of different heights and widths in a straight line with the centers of the images all at the same level.

two parallel lines

Similar to a single-line arrangement, this approach creates a unified look by arranging artwork in multiple straight lines. Start with one line, arranging the frames so that the bottoms of the frames are all level. Use this as your top row and then create a second row below it in which the tops of the frames are all level. Mount the top row approximately two inches above the bottom row.

To create stunning symmetry in a single line, alternate between tall and short frames, but make sure that the pieces on each end are similar in size.

an eclectic composition

Whether circular, square, or something in between, don't discard your mismatched frames. Bring them all together to form a unique mix-and-match collection. Confine your display to a specific area, such as the wall space over your mantel or sofa. Keeping the collection tight and unified will make it feel like showcased artwork.

Plan your composition first by cutting out smaller replicas of your frames with graph paper. Arrange your paper replicas in different designs, focusing on creating symmetry with the larger frames. Then fill in the gaps with your smaller pieces.

floating photo wall

Achieve a dramatic effect and maximize your hanging space by keeping your mats and frames the same color as your wall. Your photos and artwork will stand out from the background and appear to almost float in the air. It is a technique that works especially well if you have a large number of frames to hang on a single wall.

Single Line

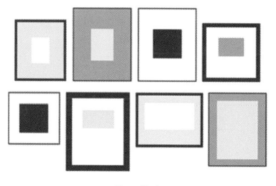

Parallel

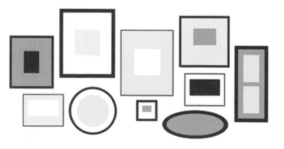

Eclectic

finalizing your arrangement

However you choose to arrange your photos, there is one smart, simple way to mount your display on the wall. If you made paper frame replicas, use Scotch tape to attach them to a piece of paper or poster board representing your wall. You can also create a quick sketch on a piece of paper. Using this as a guide, lay your artwork on the floor in the same way and then use a tape measure and pencil to lightly mark where each frame goes on the wall.

measuring and mounting your frames

When hanging frames that are held up by wire, save yourself time and energy by predetermining how the frame will lie against the wall:

1. Pull the wire as tightly as you can toward the top of the frame. Measure from your finger holding the wire to the top of the frame.

2. Hold the picture where you want it on the wall. Mark the wall at the top of the frame.

3. Measure from your mark down the wall to the distance you measured in step one. Insert the nail here and hang your picture.

diamonds in the rough

With a little love, an imaginative eye, and some elbow grease, just about any piece of furniture can come back to life. While you are out perusing yard sales, thrift stores, and outdoor markets, examine potential pieces, however old or neglected, with restoration in mind. By getting creative and reinventing a forgotten furniture piece, you can stretch your home decorating dollar and add a unique handcrafted touch to your space.

what's old is new again

Many items found at yard sales, thrift shops, and even in your own home have the potential to be very useful and beautiful with a simple facelift. Focus on the bones of the piece: See past rough exteriors and look for sturdy foundations, pretty silhouettes, and unique details that add character. When you have found a furniture piece you love, let the restoration process begin.

cleaning and painting wrought iron

1. Rust can be cleaned from wrought iron using a wire brush. Wear safety glasses to keep flying debris away from your eyes. In a well-ventilated area, lay out some newspaper or cardboard to catch the rust flakes and then brush with dry bristles until completely clean.

2. Once the rust has been completely removed, apply wrought iron primer and let dry.

3. Paint wrought iron any color under the sun for a fresh new look! Spray paint works best on metals.

sanding and painting wood

1. Sanding wood makes the surface smooth so that paint can be applied. In a well-ventilated area, rub fine-grit sandpaper along the

wood grain (the natural lines that appear in the wood) until the edges and seams are smooth and old paint, stain, or sealant is removed.

2. Be sure to remove all the dust and dirt particles from the furniture before applying a fresh coat of paint. Get the job done with Swiffer. Its trap-and-lock technology removes dirt and dust wonderfully.

3. To add color, brush on water-based paint or stain, or wood-specific spray paint.

4. After the paint or stain has dried, apply two coats of clear-coat sealer to protect and seal the color. Allow to dry fully before touching or reapplying.

cleaning and conditioning finished leather

1. Cleaning can change the color or appearance of the leather. Always test the cleaner on a small patch of leather before proceeding.

2. Add a small amount of a gentle, moisturizing soap to a damp cloth and bring it to a light lather. Rub the cloth on the leather using a small amount of water.

3. Wipe away the lather with a damp cloth.

4. Once dry, polish with a dry towel and treat the leather with a conditioner. To change the color of the leather, look for a tinted conditioner or stain.

repurposing wrought iron and metals

1. Add hooks to a restored piece of iron or metal outdoor fencing to create your own hanging or wall-mounted pot rack. Use it to hang coats, hats, or towels, too.

2. Attach metal grates (or other metal pieces that have slats) to the wall to hold photos, decorative cards, or artwork.

3. Ornate pieces of wrought iron can make beautiful wall art on their own. Hang smaller pieces together in a cluster. For larger pieces, place against a painted wall so that the color shows through the spaces.

> Put your bed in the spotlight by repurposing a piece of wrought iron trim as a one-of-a-kind headboard. Mount it on the wall behind the bed or, if it's large enough, simply rest it on the floor.

repurposing vintage fabric

1. Vintage kimonos and saris are beautiful collectibles and can be used as decoration by hanging them on your wall as is. If their condition won't allow for that, consider making place mats or covering old throw pillows.

2. Wrap a canvas in vintage tablecloths or aprons as kitchen décor. Pull the fabric around the canvas and staple it to the back so that the pattern is centered on the front.

3. Use repurposed fabric pieces to cover a journal or update a lampshade. If using older, fragile fabric, be sure to use a lower watt or

lower heat lightbulb to avoid potentially overheating or discoloring the fabric.

repurposing wooden pieces

1. Old or outdated dressers and bureau pieces can be repurposed in the kitchen or dining area for dish and linen storage. Use paint or stain to brighten them up so that they coordinate with your existing décor.

2. Use old fruit crates or wooden boxes as shelving. Be sure to use hardware that will adequately support the weight you will be adding to the wall; using at least one wall stud will provide the best support. Attach the bottom of the crate to the wall so that the opening faces outward. Place some in your kitchen to display items or to store spices, jars, and cookbooks.

3. Jewelry boxes with lots of drawers are a smart way to organize and store cosmetics in the bathroom.

4. Take interesting refurbished stools, benches, and wooden chairs to use as plant stands in sunny spots throughout your space.

5. Use an old wooden coat tree to track the height of your little ones. Give the tree a fresh coat of paint and attach paper cutouts marked with "age" and "date" so you can mark their heights as they grow.

6. Spruce up an old entertainment center with a fresh coat of paint and new hardware to create a sophisticated storage piece. Its large, deep compartments are perfect for stowing electronics, books, and toys.

repurposing leather pieces

1. Leather suitcases or travel bags can be decorative and functional. Try using them as magazine or paperwork holders in your living room or office.

2. Use thin or skinny leather belts or straps as ties for draperies.

3. Use a collection of old watches with leather straps as striking napkin rings.

One of the great things about owning a home is thinking about how you'd like to decorate it if money weren't an object. Almost all of us have some plans, ideas, or dreams of updating the look in at least one of our rooms, but many times these plans are put off because the intended changes seem too major.

Jump-start your space makeover with a few décor projects that aren't major. You can complete them in a weekend or less. Plus, they're the kinds of changes you could make in an apartment or rental house without risking too much.

Begin by obtaining your supplies at a hardware store or home center on Friday, perhaps while you're running errands or on your way home from work. Then complete the projects on Saturday and leave Sunday for anything left over, such as cleaning up and adding finishing touches.

replacing light switch plates

One of the easiest ways to update the look in a room is to update the light switches. It is usually the first thing you reach for when you walk into a room, so a new switch plate will surely get noticed.

Find a decorative switch plate that will fit the design of the rest of your room. Replace a plastic plate with one of brass, copper, or chrome for a more refined and decorative look. There are even switch plates that have textured designs or pretty color schemes. Use a screwdriver to unscrew the old plate and then screw in the new one.

hanging new artwork

A very dramatic—and very simple—way to update your décor is by hanging some new artwork on the walls. Many home stores sell reproductions of famous paintings and photographs, or you can look through your own photo albums for snapshots worthy of showcasing. For tips on safely hanging and beautifully arranging your artwork and framed photographs, read Artfully Arranged Artwork on page 271.

add an accent wall

A slightly more involved decorating project than the ones above is to paint one wall in a room a different color. This accent wall is an easy way to add vibrancy to a room.

When you choose the wall that you're going to turn into an accent wall, decide what the best feature in the room is and use paint to bring that out even more. It should probably be the focal point of the room, such as a wall with a fireplace or a great piece of art on it.

Take a look around your room and figure out what the dominant color in the room is. Then use our Color Made Simple section on page 53 to choose a color that's complementary to that color.

Sometimes it is difficult to decide on a single accent color for your space. If you are torn between two or three hues, you can incorporate all of them by painting bold bands of color across your wall. Use painter's tape to create broad stripes and double-check with a level to be sure your lines are straight. Paint your desired colors in between the tape strips, let dry, and then remove—and you'll have a wall that's all your own.

> When painting an accent wall, use a small roller to avoid wasting paint. A bigger roller will absorb more paint.

> If you would rather use the metal hardware you already have, but it's looking a little dingy, remove it and make it shine again with steel wool.

replacing your bathroom hardware

Another simple redecorating project is to update the hardware in a bathroom. Cabinet knobs and drawer pulls are simple to replace and can give the bathroom a different look. These updates will also bring a new look to your kitchen. All you need is a screwdriver to remove the old hardware and to install the new pieces.

Before you purchase new hardware, measure the distance between the screw holes on the cabinet handles and the supports on the towel bar. Be sure that the new hardware you buy matches those distances.

Cabinet and drawer knobs or handles are easy to replace. Open the cabinet or drawer, unscrew it in the back, place your new knob and handle over the existing holes, and screw them in place.

lights! color! action!

Revamping a room is as simple as 1-2-3. As you make changes to your space, keep these design principles in mind:

- **Lights!** Having the right lighting can set the proper mood for a room. Try using some amber-tinted lightbulbs in your dining room to give a warm glow to your evening meals.

- **Color!** One of the simplest and least taxing ways to redesign a space is to change its color. Painting the walls with a different color or putting up new wallpaper is a great way to transform a room and give it your own personal touch.

- **Action!** Let your personality shine through by filling your space with family photos and art that represent your passions. Using art from local artists who can give you original poignant works will put a truly unique spin on your design. It is also a good idea to shop for accessories at different stores so that you are introduced to exciting new ideas and designs while ensuring that your space is really your own.

> Stripes can manipulate the perceived size of your room. Horizontal bands will make any wall appear wider, and vertical lines lend a sense of height to low-ceilinged spaces.

black-and-white beauty

Creating a color theme is one of the easiest ways to tie a room together, and there's nothing more classic and fabulous than black and white. Use the following examples of beautifully transformed household spaces as inspiration for creating your own black-and-white theme anywhere in your home. Best of all, we'll give you helpful hints for taking on a color makeover that is not only simple but also budget-friendly.

pick a palette

Just because your color palette centers around black and white doesn't mean you can't add a burst of color here and there. Try choosing one color, such as a rich mustard yellow, to pair with your black-and-white color theme, or look for jewel tones such as bright emerald green, light sapphire blue, and rich purples or pinks. You can also never go wrong with the classic combination of black, white, and red.

a stylish space to work

Give your home office or work space a clean, modern look that inspires you to stay focused and organized without losing a sense of whimsy.

- **Furniture:** Choose a few key furniture pieces to play off one another in your color theme. The white desk chair has a rounded, modern look, while the black desk features straight lines and built-in cubbies—perfect for nestling complementary accents or using for extra organization.

- **Accents:** Mix black-and-white accents with small bits of color. For a work space make them purposeful as well—choose trays, organizers, mugs, and supplies that fit your theme.

- **Artwork:** For a fun and functional way to decorate your work space, use circular cork mats as a free-form bulletin board. Paint the mats

of various sizes in black and white and then hang them in a pattern or in an arrangement that suits your style.

lovely living space

Whether it is a nook for reading or your full living room, give your sitting areas a classically cozy look with black and white as your starting point.

- **Furniture:** Easy-to-clean fabric in dark colors such as black is perfect for living spaces that see a lot of hangout time. It won't show dirt and spills and will go with almost anything. You can also give almost any piece of furniture a coat of white paint to tie your black-and-white space together. Read Diamonds in the Rough, page 276, for tips on sanding and painting wood.

- **Accents:** Keep things simple and uncluttered with a combination of functional and decorative pieces. Accent pillows are an inexpensive way to incorporate a trendy pattern or graphic print that can easily be switched out. The same goes for lampshades: Start with a basic white base and add a fancy-looking shade that can be changed as you please.

- **Artwork:** Repaint old frames in black and white and then create your own object artwork. Choose ordinary objects in such basic shapes as keys, charms, and puzzle pieces. Paint them black or white and mount on complementary paper or poster board in a variety of shapes or designs. Add a bright complementary color to one frame and a few of your objects for added interest.

delightful dining area

Create a beautiful basic space where you can relax and enjoy a meal, quick bite, or morning coffee.

- **Furniture:** Create a snug seating area for two near a window, a cozy spot to enjoy a cup of coffee or a romantic meal. Paint a small table set that will fit your black-and-white theme. Try painting the table white and then paint the chairs solid black. You could also add some playful color on the legs or rungs.

Pay tribute to someone special with a small handmade silhouette. Make your own by taking a profile photo and then cutting around the edge of the head on the photo with a sharp craft knife. Trace the profile image onto black paper and cut it out. Mount the finished silhouette onto white or decorative paper and frame it.

- **Accents:** Make your seating soft with tie-on seat cushions in black and white. You can refresh the look whenever you like with new cushions. Light up your space with a sheer shade on a nearby window and use wall sconces in black and white to fit the café feel of the area. You can even use your place settings to bring in your color theme: Mix and match style and color with a focus on black and white but with one bright color as an accent.

- **Artwork:** Since the focus is on the window and lighting, add art as an extra accent. Layer framed images or prints against a wall on the floor nearby. It will help give your space a casual eclectic feel.

Whether it is a peaceful mountaintop, an exotic desert, a sunny beach, or the New England coast, we all have a treasured getaway—a natural retreat where we feel most at peace. That said, why not bring that feeling inside your home? These simple inspired ideas for colors, sounds, and scents make it easy for you to create your own favorite escape to enjoy day in and day out.

rustic rockies

If you dream of a peaceful cabin perched among snow-filled peaks, bring the bold, natural look of the Rocky Mountains into your home.

- **Floor:** Woven area rugs or traditional hooked rugs
- **Walls:** Light blues, crisp whites, and dusky roses
- **Lighting:** Stately but spare statements such as a large wrought iron chandelier
- **Accents:** Artwork in metal frames and Western-inspired, wooden sculptures
- **Colors:** Soft, natural tones such as creams, tans, browns, and blues, plus bold hues such as burnt red and mustard yellow
- **Sounds:** Acoustic singer-songwriter tunes or albums featuring the sounds of nature, such as coyotes howling and mountain streams babbling
- **Scents:** Dry, sweet aromas such as juniper, cedar, anise, sage, cypress, and eucalyptus

southwestern sunset

Are you inspired by the warm hues and striking shapes of Santa Fe? With a few easy touches you can add some Southwestern spice to your home.

- **Floor:** Cool ceramic surfaces such as terra-cotta tile or flagstone

- **Walls:** Warm neutral colors plus a single bold accent hue or textured, adobe-inspired walls

- **Lighting:** Copper light fixtures or lamps with hand-stitched shades

- **Accents:** Scenic black-and-white photography, Southwestern artwork, handmade pottery, and glass vases filled with natural gemstones

- **Colors:** Deep, earthy hues such as browns, camel-beiges, and burnt oranges and reds, plus accents in bright white, turquoise, and gray

- **Sounds:** Wind sounds or Native American–inspired instrumental music

- **Scents:** Light, spicy aromas of desert sage, aloe, and dried botanicals

island paradise

Blue water, white sand, a gentle breeze, and the sound of waves crashing: It is a scene that's always soothing and inspiring. With a few oceanic elements, you can create a tropical oasis right in your living room.

- **Floor:** Marble, terrazzo, ceramic, or bamboo

- **Walls:** From pastel pink to bright yellow, bold colors reminiscent of art deco buildings in South Beach

- **Lighting:** Ceiling fans with light fixtures that feature palm leaves or natural fibers for blades

- **Accents:** Natural textures like rattan, teak, and bamboo plus tropical flowers in oversized vases and accents of seashells and natural coral

- **Colors:** Bright blues, teals, fuchsia pinks, corals, bright yellows, and lime greens

- **Sounds:** Authentic Cuban music or the sounds of ocean waves and winds

- **Scents:** Energetic aromas such as citrus, spices, ocean breezes, and tropical flowers

cape cod cottage

Lobster bakes, lighthouses, colonial architecture, and a nod to shabby chic define the Cape Cod style. Make it all your own with easy ideas that turn your home into a New England getaway.

- **Floor:** Tile or whitewashed hardwood

- **Walls:** Barely-there pastels or tone-on-tone whites and creams

- **Lighting:** Ornate crystal chandelier or mix-and-match lamps in various sizes, shapes, and lampshade patterns

- **Accents:** Throws, pillows, and slipcovers in coordinating floral patterns plus Nantucket-style baskets, seashells, antiques, and wicker furniture

- **Colors:** Light, airy hues, from robin's egg blue to powder pink plus antique white, Nantucket red accents, and bold-colored floral patterns

- **Sounds:** Albums featuring the sounds of ocean waves, thunderstorms, and a crackling fire

- **Scents:** Fresh, clean scents like summer rain or linens swinging on the clothesline

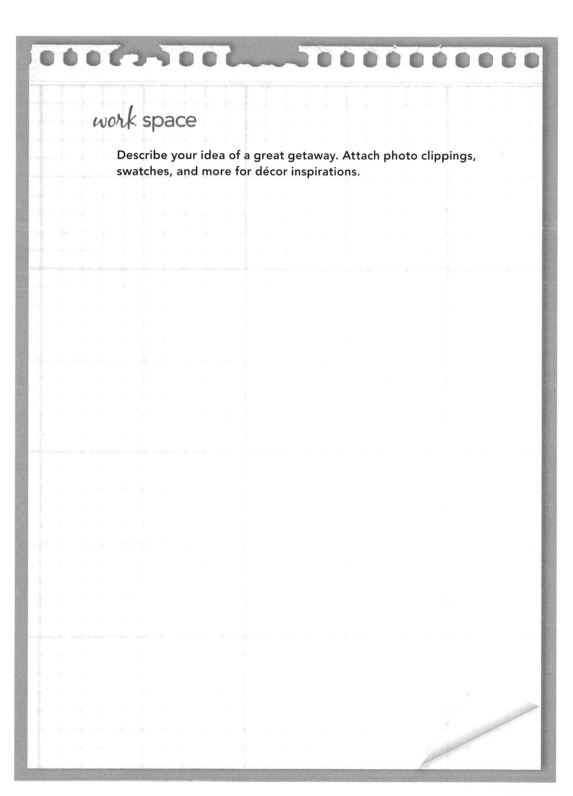

work space

Describe your idea of a great getaway. Attach photo clippings, swatches, and more for décor inspirations.

bedroom makeovers

Between resting and beautifying every day, we spend a lot of time in our bedrooms. Yet, surprisingly, when it comes to décor, bedrooms are one of the most overlooked spaces in our home. Even though it may not be a place you show off to your guests, it should still be a room you love to be in—and that doesn't have to mean drastic changes. You can personalize this space into a dreamy place with a few simple additions.

sleeping 'n' such

If you use your bedroom as a sleep sanctuary, focus on making it as comfortable as you can. Comfort is key here, and it's all about smart choices for your bedding. Follow these tips to sweet dreams.

- **Cozy Quilt:** Dig out your family quilt or invest in a well-made one. Cotton breathes perfectly, so you never wake up too hot, yet its warm layers protect you from the cold. It's an easy item to find at department stores, but authentic ones can be found at antique shops as well. Antique quilts from the 1960s and earlier are very durable, and knowing that they're handmade with love and care gives them an even more comforting feel.

- **Feel-Good Fabrics:** Use soft, plush fabrics that feel good against your skin. Also consider the season: Try flannels for cold seasons and high-thread-count cotton for warm ones.

- **Lush Layers:** Don't be afraid to indulge in extra layers so that your bedding has a fluffiness you can really get lost in. Try extra pillows made with down feathers and even a pillow top for your mattress.

- **Calm and Cool:** For a color palette, try cool pastels such as minty greens and baby blues. These calming shades will help you feel more relaxed at bedtime.

> For fabrics that feel especially soft, use a tennis ball in your dry cycle. It fluffs your sheets as they bounce around the dryer. It also helps fabrics dry faster by keeping the fabric free from hard-to-dry tangles.

personal lounge

Do you read, journal, or watch TV in your bedroom? If you do as much thinking as you do sleeping in this space, make it easy to do the things you enjoy there. Here we'll focus on function and convenience.

- **Smart Nightstand:** Consider the function of your nightstand. It is probably where you keep your favorite reading material, TV remote, and more. If your bedside table doesn't leave much room for organizing personal items, exchange it for a nightstand or a small bookshelf that can hold everything you need.

- **Stock Supplies:** Store what you need by your bedside. Make a place in your nightstand for lots of books, a note pad, paper, pens, and whatever else you use during a long reading session. You can even add a basket for organizing the smaller items.

- **Functional Furniture:** If you have room, consider adding other pieces of furniture for specific purposes. For example, keep a shelf or chest with your favorite movies or consider a small recliner for an alternate place to read. Also keep a breakfast tray nearby, such as under the bed, to use as a writing surface or for resting your laptop.

- **Think Purple:** Rich shades of purple, violet, and lavender have a surprisingly strong effect on our ability to focus and think. Purple is associated with wisdom, memory, imagination, and strategic thinking, which means it's a perfect color for the place where you read and write most.

sweet retreat

If your bedroom is your favorite getaway spot, consider these ideas for transforming it into a retreat that you can really indulge in. Think textures, lighting, and scents. Keep your linens fresh and great-smelling with Febreze products. The best part is that they won't stain delicate fabrics.

- **Luxury Feel:** Find sensational textures such as high-thread-count sheets and down comforters. Silk is a little more difficult to maintain, but using accents, such as pillowcases and a single sheet, give you the silk feel without the work—or the price—of the whole set.

- **Spa Style:** To give your bedroom a spa-like look, use wall colors that are reminiscent of a spa setting such as pale pinks for a feminine palette and greens for a Zen feel.

- **Soft Looks:** Soft lighting will help you set a mood. Look for lamps that diffuse light nicely and use white, low-wattage lightbulbs.

- **Heaven Scent:** Surrounding yourself with your favorite scent can help you relax and rejuvenate. Introduce aromatherapy into your bedroom through diffusers and flameless candles. These are both stylish and safe to leave unattended as you fall asleep.

unexpected décor

When you visit a home, it's the unique and unexpected touches that really make it a memorable space. Whether you incorporate boldly patterned wallpaper, bright rugs, or a repurposed accent piece, try bringing an eclectic energy into your home by making daring changes in small, simple ways. You may even surprise yourself!

easily transform your walls

Making changes to your wall space can be surprisingly simple. Go beyond picture frames to make lively transformations in stylish, yet manageable ways. Here are a few ideas:

- **Accent with wallpaper.** Wallpaper is back, but not the way it used to be. Today's wallpaper comes in colorful bold patterns that make a big statement in small amounts. Use it in simple panels to highlight areas such as a breakfast nook, the back of a bookshelf, or along a wall. You can also use it as a surprising element in enclosed spaces such as a kitchen pantry or medicine cabinet.

- **Create detail with wall decals.** Instead of a wall-to-wall covering such as wallpaper, wall decals are individually shaped designs and illustrations that you can apply easily wherever you'd like to add special detail to a painted wall. Some decals are design elements while others are silhouettes of animals, plants, or even cityscapes. A single decal creates a touch of interest, or you can group several to form a pattern.

- **Add dimension.** A few interesting objects or sculptural pieces can really pop. Sconce light fixtures or candleholders break up large, empty spaces in the day, and by night they shine soft light patterns across the wall. Sculptural wall accents, such as mirrors, animal shapes, or plants, offer more natural light, colors, and interesting shapes.

If you feel daring (and you should), use some bold wallpaper to re-cover an outdated fridge. You can do this using rubber cement, so the process is reversible if you decide to change your décor.

Wall decals are available for purchase online and can be found easily by entering "wall decals" in your favorite search engine.

bring garden furniture inside

Bring a little outdoor beauty into your living space. Metal garden furniture is a great way to add interest in a living room, bathroom, or any nook around your home that needs a little more life. Depending on your décor, a weathered appearance may be perfect, or you can easily repaint the item for a more polished look. Don't be afraid to try a bold color! Read Diamonds in the Rough on page 276 for tips on sanding and painting wood. Here are a few types of furniture you may like to use:

- **Plant Stands:** Tiered plant stands make great unconventional organizers. Use one in the bedroom for a decorative shoe rack and another in the bathroom to hold such items as brushes, curling irons, and blow-dryers. Or you can try a more traditional use: Put your house plants on a pedestal to make your indoor greenery a true focal point.

- **Metal Lawn Chairs:** A 1950s-style metal chair is a nice vintage touch, and most are surprisingly comfortable—especially when you use a decorative pillow to soften the seat.

- **Garden Accessories:** You can repurpose outdoor accessories in unexpected ways. For accent furniture, a gardener's cart can be used as a buffet table and a sundial stand can be used as an end table.

> If you are adding a new color or pattern to a room, try adding it in three places to help tie everything together. Remember to trust your own eye and use your creativity!

create unexpected end tables

You can never have enough places to set your drink or rest your favorite magazine between readings. But you don't have to spend a lot of cash at furniture stores. Instead, you can create more surfaces by stacking interesting items that can be found around your home or purchased inexpensively. Here are a few examples:

- **Suitcases:** You can often find small vintage travel cases in local antique shops and thrift stores. They come in such fun colors as aqua, olive, rich browns, and tans. Stack two or three from largest to smallest for a nostalgic coffee table or end table that doubles as storage.

- **Hatboxes:** These are also stackable items. Try stacking two to four, depending on their size. Also, don't be afraid to mix new and old boxes or solid colors and patterns.

throw down bright, bold rugs

Rugs add lots of color and take minimal effort. Have fun with your options. Modern patterns are bold and stylish, while polka dots are classic and playful. Or you can go wild with an animal print. The best part is that there's no handiwork involved. You just have to find the perfect spot. Here are some places where a bright rug may work for you:

- **Doorways:** Welcome your guests by making a statement right at the door. Place a colorful mat on your doorstep. It will make a great first impression and help prevent mud and grass stains from being tracked onto your interior rugs. For unique, create-your-own options for welcome mats, read A Welcoming Touch for Your Front Door on page 247.

- **Understated Areas:** Turn any space from neutral to noticeable by creating a focal point with a large patterned rug.

- **Passageways:** Try a bold runner up steps or down a hallway. Even places where you don't linger can make a memorable space.

family-style décor

There is family-style dining, so why not family-style décor? Decorating with the objects that remind you of the important people in your life is a heartwarming way to enhance the look of your home. Try a few of our clever ways to show off your family treasures.

central spot for special mementos

Create one area in your home that reflects your family's history and accomplishments. Choose a place that you'll see every day, such as a wall in the front hallway or part of the living room. Then pull together the family mementos that make you smile.

Trophies, photos, arts and crafts from your children or grandchildren, and heirlooms from your ancestors are what you are looking for. Choose your favorite mementos so that this area doesn't get too cluttered.

creating a unified look

Turn your family photos into a cohesive collection by printing all of them in black and white or in sepia tones. Framing your pictures in similar frame colors or styles will also give your photos a professional finish.

Another way to bring out the beauty of your family photographs is to enlarge them. Enlarging your favorite snapshots into 8 × 10 black-and-white photos and putting them in stylish frames creates a beautiful artistic look to favorite family moments.

The great thing about children's artwork is how unique each piece is. You can really see the difference in their artistic skills as they get older. Using similar frames for their favorite pieces will help you create a unified look for the whole collection. Hang them alongside your family pictures and replace the artwork when the kids come home with newer pieces.

larger pieces

Not all family treasures can go on a wall. Some of your children's larger crafts, trophies, and other family heirlooms also need a place to call home. If you have only a few of these pieces, set up a table against the wall filled with family pictures and artwork, and arrange your mementos on top of the table.

If you have more than a few trophies or family heirlooms that you want to share, install a few designer shelves. You can hang your photos and artwork around, between, and among the shelves.

box full of memories

To display smaller pieces like medals, old tickets, vacation souvenirs, old jewelry, and toys from your childhood, create a shadowbox. You can use this home décor accessory to display all sorts of collections.

Materials

Paint and paintbrush
Wooden box or sturdy gift box
Decorative fabric
Spray adhesive

Hot glue
Favorite mementos
Hammer and nails

Instructions

1. Choose a paint that will go well with the rest of your collection as well as your room's décor, and then paint the outside of the box.

2. Cut the fabric to fit the interior bottom of the box and then spray the adhesive on both the cloth and the bottom of the box. When the adhesive gets tacky, carefully press the cloth flatly to the bottom.

3. Repeat the step above with the four interior sides of the box.

4. Use the hot glue to attach the mementos artfully inside the shadowbox.

5. Use the hammer and nails to hang the shadowbox on a wall along with your pictures and artwork.

knockout colors

Sometimes a nook or corner of your home "just needs a little something." Simple! Create interest in special areas by using paint instead of purchasing new furniture or working to rearrange what you already have. Get inspired with our ideas for flooding color into unexpected places and discover that you really can pack a big punch with a little paint. All you need are your household painting supplies and free afternoon.

architectural highlights

Glance around your space. What does your family consider its architectural treasures? By adding more color contrast you can really catch eyes and showcase them in ways they've never been shown off before.

- **Colorful Alcoves and Arches:** Give recessed windows, curvy doorway arches, and hard-to-notice nooks more attention with a fresh coat of paint. Try tones that are subtly different from the rest of the room since you want the objects, not the color, to be the focus. Choosing a lighter shade over a darker one for recessed areas will also ensure that they don't get lost in the shadows. For everything you need to know about perfecting your paint job, see Perfect Paint Jobs on page 263.

- **Emphasized Slants:** Vaulted ceilings in a great room or dormered ceilings in a bedroom are interesting features you definitely don't want to see fall flat. Help them stand out from your walls by making them the highlight of the room. Give them a coat of bright, crisp white. The fresh paint will catch light from windows and leave your space more airy and open.

- **New View:** If you have a window you really love, try painting its trim a contrasting shade. Choosing a color that really stands out from the wall will draw the eye right in. This is a great way to frame a beautiful view.

bold floods

For spaces that don't already have an architectural focus, create one with your favorite color. Choose a unique color that you love in small doses. You will have a spot to use those rich shades that would probably be too much on a whole wall.

- **Accented Ceiling:** Rich or dark colors can make a room look smaller, but not if you paint the ceiling. Take a small area, like a half bath, utility room, or short hallway, and use your accent color above. Try something bright for a cheery feel or something bold to make a stylish statement. This is the perfect way to draw more attention to an interesting light fixture, too.

- **Backsplash of Color:** Using light colors makes a space feel larger, which may be the approach you used in your kitchen. If so, there is still room for color, especially if you don't have backsplash tile. Paint the space between your upper cabinets and countertops with an appetizing shade such as red, orange, eggplant purple, or warm brown. Do you have under-cabinet lighting? Even better! Turn it on and watch your new backsplash of color glow.

peek-a-boo brights

If painting large areas isn't for you, try adding hints of vibrant colors in hidden or often ignored places instead. It is a thoughtful touch that says you spent time making your space unique to you. It also adds an element of surprise where guests least expect it.

- **Unexpected Spots:** Does your room have an interesting accent color? Paint the drawers in it. Look for inspiration in the details of the room. In your bedroom it may be the boldest color in the pattern on your bed linens. For a kid's room try a different color for every drawer. In a living room you may have a vase or other accent piece that inspires you. Paint the entryway closet that color. Brightly painted drawer interiors, cabinets, and closets aren't just fun—they make staying organized a little more enjoyable, too.

- **Edgy Edges:** Highlight the dimension of some of your favorite objects by painting their edges. It is a great way to add color to wooden elements. Try the edges of a wooden table or the sides of

> Use highly durable kitchen and bathroom paint for areas that are exposed to water splashes, steam, grease, and more. That way, they won't smudge permanently. All you have to do is wipe the messes away.

a picture frame. It also creates interest for neutrally painted items, too. For example, paint a bright shade at the back of a bookcase. For a staircase that is already painted, try coloring every other spindle for a fun effect.

colorful floors

If you have wood or linoleum floors, think beyond painting just your walls or trim. You can paint areas of your hard floor, too. All you have to do is very thoroughly clean the area that you want to color and apply several layers of paint to protect it from the wear and tear of foot traffic.

- **Grounded in Color:** Forget finding a rug with the right size and shape. Stenciling an "area rug" or a border on the floor is a great way to break up space without an expensive floor covering. Try it under a table or as a border for embellishment in a more formal room.

- **Run With It:** Here are some smart ideas if your stairs are worn or could just use some color. Paint a "runner" up a wooden staircase for a sophisticated touch or paint entire steps in alternating colors for a more whimsical look.

> **Choosing the right materials will be key to the durability of your floor design. Pick paint that was made for floors. You may also consider applying a clear top coat. Talk to the knowledgeable people at your local hardware store for the best advice about your particular floor type.**

mirror, mirror

Mirrors aren't just for applying eyeliner anymore. There are many ways you can use them around your home to create interest, the illusion of space, and extra light. They are also inexpensive items that are easy to find at any home store or thrift shop. They come in so many shapes, sizes, and frame styles that the possibilities are endless. Try these tips to incorporate mirrors in your home.

mirrors that function

- **Reflective Trivets:** Repurpose small mirrors as trivets on your dinner table. They will dress up your dish and protect your table from heat. Look for mirrors with interesting and irregular edges. They can have frames but it is preferable that they don't. Instead, look for options that are beautifully beveled around the edges.

  Trivets are also a great way to repurpose an old mirror that is too distressed to use anymore. The discoloration and texture of the silver behind the glass gives an endearing vintage look. And if you are buying the mirror, you can probably get a deal on the price. No matter what kind of mirror you choose, just remember to attach some small rubber pads on the bottom. They help keep the trivet in place and prevent it from scratching the surface of the table. Look for rubber pads where furniture pads are sold at your local hardware store.

- **Twinkling Candlescape:** This is the perfect surface to light a cluster of candles. A mirror reflects the soft, flickering light, and it's easy to remove wax from it, too. For this idea, choose medium-size mirrors rather than small ones. Again, you can opt for a frame or no frame. If you do use a mirror with a frame, consider painting it to match your décor. And if you're feeling artistic, you can even paint a pattern on the glass, letting the reflective surface shine through. For ideas about how to build a tablescape with your new candle platform, see One-Two-Three Tablescapes on page 74.

If you use paint on your candlescape surface, remember to read the instructions. Avoid paints that are flammable. Also let the painted surface dry thoroughly before placing a lit candle on top.

mirrors for beauty

One large mirror is a great way to fill wall space, but a collection of small mirrors adds more interest and visual texture—and often will cost less. Follow these steps to create your own display.

Materials

5 to 7 mirrors
Glossy interior paint
Paintbrush
Blue painter's tape
Nails

Hammer
Picture hardware of your choice (if needed)
All-purpose cleaner
Paper towels or a lint-free towel

Instructions

1. Choose an open wall in your home where you'd like to create more interest.

2. Collect five to seven small or medium mirrors at local secondhand stores.

3. Paint all the frames one color. To avoid accidentally painting the face of the mirror, tuck pieces of blue tape between the frame and the mirror itself. If you do get a dab or two on the glass, don't worry. Simply let it dry and then scratch it off with your fingernail or a plastic putty knife.

4. Clean each mirror to a beautiful shine with your all-purpose cleaner and a paper towel.

5. Decide how you will arrange the mirrors. You can practice on the floor in front of the chosen wall. This will help you judge spacing more easily. For ideas about how to hang your collection artfully, see Artfully Arranged Artwork on page 271.

6. Now you are ready to hang with your hammer and nails and enjoy!

mirrors for space

Do you have a mirror that you love just the way it is? All you have to do is consider how and where to place it. It can open up a room in many ways. Check out these ideas for maximizing the benefits of your mirror just by hanging it in a smart spot:

- **Hall Mirror:** Try placing your favorite mirror at the end of a hallway. You'll be surprised to see how it creates the illusion that the space extends farther. Depending on the size and height of your mirror, it can really elongate the appearance of the hall.

- **Multimirror, Multitasking:** Place several mirrors in a shared bathroom so that no one has to wait to look good. Another idea is to add one beside the door you use the most. That way you can always make sure you look your best before heading out for the day.

- **Let There Be Light:** Place a mirror across from a window in one of your darkest rooms. Be sure it is positioned in a way that allows it to catch the most light. Just think: A single mirror can almost double the amount of light in that space!

do-it-yourself flower power

Fresh professional floral arrangements are beautiful, but they can also be very expensive. Fortunately, that doesn't have to mean fresh flowers aren't for you. Instead of ordering from a florist, use this helpful how-to for creating wonderful—and wonderfully inexpensive—floral designs at home year-around.

select your stems

Flowers alone are surprisingly affordable. That is because much of the cost of an arrangement comes from the cost of the container and the floral designer's time. This means that if you buy them loose, you save! The first step is finding them. Loose flowers aren't too hard to come by as long as you know where to look.

- **When You Are Short on Time:** When you need a floral touch in a flash, check your local grocery store. You should be able to find roses, spider mums, and alstroemeria year-round as well as seasonal selections such as tulips in the spring and sunflowers in the fall.

- **Planning Ahead:** When you have a little more time to work with, consider ordering more unusual varieties from your local florist. They will be more than happy to help you find flowers that match your personal style. With these starter ideas you will be able to make a floral statement for a lot less than you think.

convenient containers

The first thing you're going to need is a vase to arrange your flowers. You don't have to spend much or maybe even anything at all. If you have saved vases from past arrangements, check the stash you already have. If you can't find the look you're going for at home, try a thrift store or discount store before paying full price at a craft or home décor retailer.

Before settling on a vase, decide what you'd like to do with it and how many of the containers you will need. Wash your containers with Dawn to give them a brilliant shine that really shows off the blooms.

three floral ideas

Whether you use a single flower in multiple vases or multiple flowers in a single vase, home-designed flowers can be just as impressive as professional arrangements. Here are a few different looks and advice that will help you make it happen.

1. **Flowerscape:** For a maximum look with minimal flowers, consider using three single stems and three small vases. Flowers that work best for this have full faces and long, strong necks. Gerbera daisies are a casual and fun choice and come in almost every color. Peonies are classic. Spider chrysanthemums are sophisticated and very inexpensive. For a bold, contemporary look, ask your florist for pincushion proteas.

   Now consider the space where you'll display your mini arrangements. For long spaces, such as tables and mantels, use three to five of the same vase and arrange them in a generously spaced row. For a round or square space, cluster three containers of slightly different heights.

2. **Large and in Charge:** If you are looking for a focal point, such as a centerpiece, choose flowers with natural height. Try classic and fragrant stock, which comes in a wide array of colors. For a chic green look, use Bells of Ireland. Cymbidium orchids are a little more expensive, but their exquisite blooms are worth it for a more formal occasion.

   Once you have your stems, simply group three or five together, placing each at a slight angle so they hold one another up. If your style is more minimalist, try curly willow branches. They are cool and contemporary. You will need five to ten of these and will want to put them in the vase all at once, straight up and down, fluffing them up as you tuck.

3. **Hip to Be Square:** For a mixed flower style, try finding a square or rectangular vase. They look fresh, and they're easier for beginners to use than vases with round openings. Start with two or three

Flowers always make a thoughtful gift. Use extra vases you've collected through the years or purchase inexpensive ones that the recipients can keep. This is less expensive than having flowers delivered and more personal, too!

stems of large white or green hydrangeas. Cut them so they sit just above and cover the vase opening.

Next, using the hydrangeas for support, add five to seven stems of another flower of your choice. Try roses for a traditional look, calla lilies for a more sophisticated arrangement, or hypericum berries for a simple finish with a touch of texture. All are available in many colors, so you can match your décor or the season. Simply tie a bow around the vase, and you're ready to showcase your custom floral design.

work space

Some flowers have funny names that are hard to remember.
Keep a working list of your favorites here.

Flower	Season	Colors	Shop	Notes

Placing a simple glass vase on a table, counter, or elsewhere can transform a space instantly. But it's what you put in the vase that truly makes it a standout piece. There are many options that are less expensive and more creative than flowers. Below are ten inspiring suggestions for filling a vase in ways that will take your space from standard to sublime any time of year.

vase variety

An empty glass vase is just waiting for you to fill with your own personal sense of style and creativity. There are so many shapes and styles of vases to choose from: cylinders, squares, curvy, or classic. Whether you have a collection of vases from floral deliveries or have found a few deals at your local home goods store, simple glass vases offer a budget-friendly opportunity to renew your décor.

Use these ten ideas as a starting point and let your imagination transform a vase before your eyes:

1. **Fruit Filled:** Use real or artificial fruit to add a burst of fresh color to your room. Green apples, clementines, lemons, and limes are all good choices because they don't need refrigeration. Layer fruits with different colors and textures in a wide-mouthed vase or use one fruit type for a clean, modern look.

2. **Lots of Moss:** Moss is often used as filler or an accent inside a vase with other plants or flowers. Instead, try filling an entire vase with fuzzy green texture. For a unified motif, fill vases of different sizes and shapes with layers of moss and place them throughout a room.

3. **Pretty Plumes:** Create an arrangement in a cylinder vase using tall, fancy feathers such as from a peacock or ostrich. Choose bright colors or neutrals depending on your overall décor. Use feathers of varying sizes and heights to mimic the look of a floral arrangement.

Any of these vase ideas can be repurposed as a beautiful centerpiece for your table. Try creating your own unique design by filling a vase based on the theme of your dinner party, the occasion, or the season.

4. **Blooms Only:** Trim the blooms from fresh, dried, or artificial flowers and layer them inside a vase. The more colorful and dramatic the blossoms, the better, but classic white works well, too, especially in a busy room. You can also float a single bloom at the top of a small glass vase or dish filled with water. Add a few drops of bleach to help preserve it.

5. **Child's Play:** Décor in a playroom or family room should be colorful and quirky with a nod to the room's more casual use. Choose playful objects to layer, such as wood building blocks with letters or numbers, toy cars, board game pieces, or even multicolored bouncy balls.

6. **Coffee Color:** A vase filled with coffee beans can add a little café atmosphere to your kitchen. Use a square vase shape to juxtapose the rounded shape of the beans. Pair the rich, dark color of the beans with spring-inspired colors such as bubble-gum pink or robin's egg blue. Add the color easily with a silky ribbon tied around the vase or by setting flowers or a single candle in the center.

7. **Seasonal Sensations:** Change your décor in an instant by filling a vase with signs of the season. For spring use colorful plastic eggs or marshmallow chicks. Bright green palm leaves are perfectly beachy for summer. For fall, try pine cones or gourds. For winter, fill a vase with evergreen sprigs or shiny glass ornaments.

8. **From the Sea:** Create an island oasis with your seaside collection. Fill a tall vase with shells and coral of all shapes and sizes arranged at interesting angles. Put it on display during summer months or anytime you need a little getaway.

9. **Made for Metallic:** Make your vase shine with pretty metal objects. Coin collections, antique keys, mismatched silverware, and costume jewels can all make an elegant impression in your space. Try a short, slender vase with a wide mouth and fan out silverware around the mouth or create your own special arrangement. Place on a hutch in the dining room or use as a centerpiece for a table.

10. **Fabulous Fibers:** Yarn comes in all sorts of beautiful colors and soft textures. Filling a vase with yarn is a great way to show off your hobby or just make a room feel warm and cozy. It often comes rolled

> Create a wish tree by arranging bare branches inside a large glass vase. Cut old greeting cards into squares and have family or friends write down their wishes. Then attach the wishes to the tree with ribbon or small clips.

in fun formations or balls, so try layering your yarn in its unused form or create an arrangement with loose scraps you've hung on to. Finish off the look with a pair of simple silver knitting needles poking out at the top. Be sure to display it on a high shelf or mantel if you have little ones around.

conclusion

We hope our book has a special place in your life and home for years to come, whether you keep it on your coffee table, in your bookshelf, or at your bedside. Use the inspiration you've found in these pages and the ideas you've jotted down to make your home a beautiful place and your life a little easier every day.

If you love the tips, projects, and recipes from our book, we invite you to join us online at HomeMadeSimple.com for more fresh ideas to make your own. Sign up and log in to enhance your experience and get our inspiring e-mails delivered straight to your in-box.

At Home Made Simple, we love finding innovative solutions to help you create the home you love to live in, so be on the lookout for more great offerings from us online, in print, on TV, and beyond!

index